1992

THE ART OF LEARNING

The Art of Learning

*A Self-Help Manual
for Students*

Katherine M. Ramsland

State University
of New York Press

Published by
State University of New York Press, Albany

Printed in the United States of America

Production by Bernadine Dawes
Marketing by Dana Yanulovich

For information, address the State University of New York Press,
State University Plaza, Albany, NY 12246

Library of Congress Cataloging-in-Publication Data

Ramsland, Katherine M., 1953-
    The art of learning : a self-help manual for students / Katherine
M. Ramsland.
        p.   cm.
    Includes bibliographical references (p.   ) and index.
    ISBN 0-7914-0921-X (alk, paper) : $29.50. -- ISBN 0-7914-0922-8
(pbk. : alk. paper) : $9.95
    1. Learning, Psychology of. 2. Thought and thinking. 3. Study,
Method of.   I.   Title.
LB1060.R35   1992

370.15'23-dc20   91-15155
                                                        CIP

10 9 8 7 6 5 4 3 2 1

Contents

Introduction

The first time I got on a toboggan, I was scared.

"It'll be great!" I was promised. I swallowed my fear and climbed on the front. Two of my friends sat giggling behind me. I had no idea how to steer, so I just pulled my cap over my eyes and hoped for the best. Someone handed me the rope and gave us a push. The toboggan whizzed down the hill, picking up speed. I clung to the rope, seeing nothing through my cap and just praying for the ride to be over quickly.

It was. All too quickly. Near the bottom, the unchecked toboggan changed course and crashed into a tree, breaking my arm and leg. Had I been steering, in all likelihood the accident would have been prevented.

Being "along for the ride" is just as risky for a college student. It may happen that some students will glide through without a scratch, but they may miss much of the thrill of the ride that comes from seeing where you're going, feeling the sense of control and attending to the moment-by-moment experience.

In this book I encourage you as a student to get back to the basics of what it means to *be* a student, not so much in terms of the skills of reading and writing, as in *attitude*. All too often it is simply assumed that all you have to do is go to the classroom with pen and paper, take and memorize notes. But this is like viewing tennis as merely going to the court with a racket and a can of balls or believing you can drive if you sit behind the steering wheel of a car. The skills involved for each of these activities are much more complicated because they are connected with who you are as a learner, and you need to develop an approach that will assist you in coordinating yourself with, and honing those skills. Many freshman entering college today are not really students in the full sense of the word. They are not ready to master any subject or skill because they do not know the fundamental steps involved. It is not unusual to hear any of the following statements:

"I feel pressured to get high grades and sometimes I concentrate so much on the grade that I don't feel I learned anything."

"It seems like all I do is memorize information. After awhile, it all blends together."

"Going to class makes me tense. I know I'm here to learn, but I also feel stressed out, so I avoid going to class."

"I hate the professor. I can't learn a thing in that course!"

Each of these statements is a symptom of the larger problem that the art of learning has lost its roots in the *learner*.

Theories of learning abound, but they are often too abstract to apply to the practical day-to-day situation of the average college student. They also are aimed primarily at the mechanics of education or they emphasize external conditions rather than the intrinsic motivational role of the learner. You are viewed as a passive recipient and the teacher as the authority in charge— not a great start to a relationship.

Some professors complain these days about the "unfriendly soil of the student's soul," meaning that they perceive you to be distrustful, wary, and unwilling to put much effort into your education. This perspective may be due in part, to the traditional assumptions of what learning is all about. It is often confused with *quantitative* changes: you had a notebook full of notes, you memorized most of it for the test and did pretty well, so you "must have learned a lot."

However, this equation is too restrictive. As an undergraduate, I took a course on attitudes toward war. We read, we discussed, and we kept journals. I had few concrete classroom notes and yet, as I read over my journal, I realized with a start that I had *changed.* I was not necessarily able to recall most of the content of the course, but my attitude about war was quite different at the end of the course than it had been at the beginning. I could point to nothing specific in the text as the cause of this change. It simply occurred. As a result, not only did I learn something important about the subject of that course, I also learned something about *learning*—that it can happen at more levels than simple rote activity, and that my own motivated involvement made an important contribution. It makes sense, then, that expanding awareness and paying more attention to the *process* as a coordination of inner and outer activities can offer you more effective methods of learning than is offered by mechanical or quantitative approaches.

There are clear indications that attitudes about education need to change. Boards of higher education are concerned at how students seem unprepared to think creatively or independently, skills they will need for their careers. "We put children in groups," says psychologist and creativity expert, Mark Runco, "and make them sit in desks and raise their hands before they talk. We put all the emphasis on conformity and order, then we wonder why they aren't being spontaneous and creative." In response to the concerns, teachers and parents are rethinking the traditional approach and are expressing the need to encourage active participation in students, even in the earliest grades.

Students, too, are showing by their actions that they are not enthralled with learning as it has been structured for them. Many people give up on learning after they leave school, claims psychologist Mihaly Csikszentmihalyi,

> because thirteen or twenty years of extrinsically motivated education is still a source of unpleasant memories. Their attention has been manipulated long enough from the outside by textbooks and teachers, and they have counted graduation as the first day of freedom.

He calls for education that begins with the student's own urge "to develop a personally meaningful sense of what one's experience is all about."

In their book, *Thinking Better,* Drs. David Lewis and James Greene make a similar statement:

> That so many learn poorly when confronted by formal study is really not at all surprising when you consider the haphazard manner in which the skills are acquired. We are never taught in any systematic way how to learn, but have to pick up the necessary techniques as a result of experience, from watching others performing certain tasks, by following rules for rote memorizing and out of mistakes we make.

It is inefficient, they point out, and potentially damaging.

Unfortunately, much educational reform is aimed at more of the same, with higher standards for the same formats and more emphasis in focus on new subject areas, like science and math. The pattern is still based on external reward systems, although there is some recognition that other learning styles may be worth considering. Yet the idea of students becoming self-reliant, self-motivated learners seems perhaps too good to be believed. The authority, then, for how and what to learn remains in the hands of the teachers and administrators.

Change, however, may be slow in coming and that is why this book is not about changing the system. It is written for *you,* to alert you to the fact that you can change *yourself* by developing your own intrinsic motivation *within* the system. The basic idea is that everything we experience is represented to us in mental form, influenced by our own perspective, and something *we* can control. Control of inner experience is the essence of mastery, because you decide the measure of personal involvement. Learning, then, becomes an activity of *inner* mastery through self-organization and self-motivation. Although I still discuss grades, lectures, writing papers, and taking notes—because this is the way the educational system will remain for years to come—the *perspective* on these items and activities will evolve away from an external orientation.

It is my intention to describe a way to achieve the sense of meaning that makes learning enjoyable, and to discover how learning, *itself,* can be a source of personal freedom. Approaching the traditional structure from a learner-centered point of view can result for you in maintaining an interest in learning, in expanding your capacity to be creative and to think independently, and in developing skills that apply as much to other life situations as they do to the classrooms.

To accomplish this new approach to the process of learning, I apply related research done on the notions of "mindfulness," visualization, and the pursuit of excellence in sports and work. Along the way, I offer opportunities for you to become actively involved with the material. There is recent evidence that a new trend in encouraging increased awareness, self-motivation and creativity in whatever you do results in a more efficient and enjoyable relationship with your tasks. This can apply to learning as well as to any other activity. Therefore, no matter what major you choose, whether you plan to take only a few classes, aim toward a four-year degree, or expect to extend your education through graduate school, realizing early that the *approach* to learning is as important as acquiring skills and information can mean the difference between "just getting by" and getting exactly what you want from your education.

It may, however, be tough going at first, trying to break old habits and learn a new perspective. There will be outside pressures to focus on externals. Teachers, parents and other students may emphasize scores, tests and grade point averages. Such pressure can drain inner motivation to simply learn and you may find yourself focusing on goals instead of process. Nevertheless, the "rope" is still in your hands. It cannot be denied that people in higher education can fail you, but that will happen only if *you* allow it. If you simply climb on the toboggan and ride it down, you may crash into a tree. But if you learn how to steer, you can have the ride of your life, no matter how many trees loom ahead. The potential is there. You must take up the rope yourself and *steer.*

"But how do I do this?" you ask.

That's what this book is about. In the first part, I discuss your preliminary preparation in getting ready to make the change effectively. You need to understand what it really means to be a student and to see how your own psychological make-up can help or hinder you. The second section focuses on actual techniques and experiences that can move you toward a more active involvement with an approach to learning centered within yourself. It emphasizes what it takes to achieve the most enjoyment and the highest quality of performance. The last part of the book winds up with your place as a learner in a larger community, with specific applications of the techniques of inner learning and a general summary. Along the way, there will be shorter summaries to assist you with keeping the most important points in mind.

However, you must be willing to *act.* Learning, itself, is an active process. In this book you will find suggestions on how to develop your capacity to connect personally with the material in order to learn. Simply reading the suggestions is not enough.

Until they are applied in your life, they will mean nothing to you. No skill is ever attained through "head knowledge" alone. Make up your mind to get involved.

You may find that the decision to try to learn in the suggested manner results in a feeling of hanging on to two ropes: the tradition that feels safe and the new approach that I am suggesting. One will pull you in one direction, the other, in the the opposite. You will have to decide to drop one and grab the other, and you will have to do this initially on faith. I can assure you that, having tried both approaches myself, and having opted for the less traditional but more self-empowering one offered in the following pages, should you choose it, you will enjoy your education more. And if you enjoy it more, you will undoubtedly become more involved and reap more benefits.

PART 1

The Art of Learning

Preliminary Preparations

1

The Will to Learn

Jennifer was eager to discover how college could benefit her. Day after day, she sat in the classroom, waiting for something her professors said to have an impact. By the end of the semester nothing dramatic had happened and she was disappointed. She approached one of her professors and asked, "Is this all there is?" The professor looked at her a moment and answered, "For you, apparently so."

As simple as it is, this story contains an important truth for all potential students to learn: you cannot depend solely on others to educate you. If you do, you are making yourself vulnerable to a system that will frustrate you with its inevitable inefficiencies and imperfections. You'll enjoy your educational experience more and get more benefit if you realize that most real education is *self*-education insofar as it is *you* who decides how much and how well you will learn.

Learning is a partnership of two or more willing minds. Your teachers can assist you with information and guidance, but much of the responsibility to learn is on your shoulders. If you welcome this responsibility, you will exercise more control over your college experience, both in and out of the classroom. Then, even if some of your instructors fail to meet *their* responsibilities in the partnership, you can still salvage the situation from *your* side.

Having more control will make you feel more fully involved, and feeling more involved will make you more enthusiastic about your education; as a result, you will not only increase your capacity to learn but will probably enjoy the process more. You will also experience a greater sense of freedom and direction. But first you must understand what the process of learning involves.

In this chapter, I will focus on the most basic ingredient in learning: motivation. Other chapters will introduce you to other skills and traits that are part of improving and deepening the learning process. The end result will be to introduce you to experiencing learning as a seemingly effortless and exciting activity in which you are so absorbed in what you are doing that you lose the feeling that you are *working* at it. You may already know that feeling in a fleeting way, but the intent of this book is to get you ready to make that experience a way of life. It is not magical but is rather the result of your physical and mental powers coordinating for top-level performance. However, there *is* hard work to be done to get you there. Take it a step at a time and do not skip any steps.

_____ Being a Student

What does it mean to be a student? Many people equate it with being "brainy," but learning has little to do with being born intellectually gifted. It has everything to do with the attitude you take in controlling and broadening your own experience as you set out to master complex information. There are skills involved. Although you have been a "student" most of your life, the skills taught to you are probably rather basic, enough to get by in the classroom and move along from one grade to the next. Perhaps you have even managed to get good grades, but it is commonly believed among education specialists that much of what you have "learned" in the traditional format you may not retain or be able to recall when you need it. "We fill students full of data," says Richard Paul, who directs a center for critical thinking in California. "But the essence of education is to use information to address new situations. We're neglecting that."

The problem is partly due to the way we understand what it means to learn, which does not account for what it means to be a student in the deeper sense of the word. True learning means to adopt an attitude of striving to integrate your mental skills toward the end of achieving competence *and quality* in what you think, say and do, and to continue to be open to broadening your perspective and understanding of the world around you. To develop as a student means to be open to the *process* of learning, as much as—perhaps even more than—to the results. The process and the goals go hand in hand, and while goals are important, so much as been said about them and so little about process—the *experience* of learning—that it is time to give the process its due.

You play a stronger role in what you get out of your college experience than you may realize. In order to keep from falling back on the unproductive expectations Jennifer expressed in the opening example, you must focus on your own attitudes and skills.

It may seem to you as if attitude is a simple thing: it's either positive or negative and obviously affects your perspective. However, that's a little too simple. Consider several different attitudes to the same task, a homework assignment in a basic English course. One student says that he is working to get it over with so he can stop worrying about it; another student says she is working to get an A on the assignment; a third student claims that doing well on the assignment is a step toward doing well in the course; and a fourth student says she is using the assignment to help her eventually to write an important novel. So you see, it is not just a matter of being positive or negative. Attitudes also play a part in the degree of interest you take in what you envision for yourself and in how you motivate yourself.

Learning what it means to become a student in the manner offered to you in this book will mean putting yourself in a position that may seem to you unnecessary. You may think you are being asked to learn something that you believe you already know. However, you may be surprised to discover that as a student, you are, in some respects, a beginner. You may know how to read a book, write a paper and even make a classroom presentation, but you undoubtedly have never been taught to master the *inner* dynamic of learning that can move you beyond the basics with which you "get by" toward a sense of true mastery and heightened experience. Keeping this goal in mind, let us look at the first step: staying motivated in the initial experience of a new situation.

_____ Motivation to Learn

It is difficult to be a beginner in an impatient society. You are pressured to learn quickly, without taking too long in the transition between first acquaintance with a subject or skill and full understanding. This is one reason why many people begin a project but fail to complete it. It is also the reason many products are inferior. The difference in quality is obvious between the chair carved out by the true artisan and one produced on an assembly line for cheap distribution. Artisans develop an intimate relationship with their products, based on care and patience. It is not just an object to them but part of themselves. There may be a difference in price, but you "get what you pay for," and that applies to your approach to education as well. The price you pay may be your own change of habits.

The question to ask yourself is whether you want short-range, immediate gains or the long-term benefits that result from the kind of commitment true artisans make to their handiwork. You must make that decision for yourself. No counselor, advisor, parent or high school teacher can tell you what you want. What I will call the art of inner learning begins with *your* desire to achieve what it can offer you.

It is not necessarily an easy decision to make. The requirements of time and effort may seem intimidating. Like defying the force of gravity in the first stages of an astronaut's liftoff, the initial steps will be the most difficult. Many students do opt for the "assembly line" approach, to the great frustration of their teachers and, eventually, of the students themselves. Why? Is it because they don't *want* to make the effort? Or is it because the educational system makes the effort seem futile? Blame has been placed on both sides, but it seems more clearly to be the case that somewhere in the whirlwind of activity calculated to get you in and out of high school and college, the art of learning has been *assumed*. Being assumed, it has been lost and many of its ingredients have been separated from one another and scattered. It is like a secret that must be rediscovered, or a missing part that needs to be reconnected.

There is no quick, easy formula. In a culture where responsibility is too easily laid on the shoulders of others, you must be reminded that a key factor in learning is motivation, and motivation is controlled from *within*.

There are many motives for going to college: You want a degree that will get you a better job and more money; your parents want you to go to college; you want to be with your friends, who are going away to college; you want to give yourself an advantage over someone else; or, perhaps some time in high school, you discovered a genuine desire to expand your knowledge. Whatever your reasons, once in college, you must develop a hunger to learn if you are to commit yourself to getting the most advantage out of being there.

All of our experiences, including what we become interested in doing, are molded by the way we think about them. In the example above, outlining various attitudes, the student who just wanted to get the assignment over with was much less involved in actually learning from it or enjoying it than the student who viewed it as a means to fulfilling one of her dreams. In that way, you exercise some control. You can create intellectual hunger by developing an attitude that feeds a desire for it, and that attitude can start with simple curiosity.

It is curiosity that will initially lead you into the classroom. You want to know what a professor will be like, how he or she will cover the subject, how much work will be involved. You may simply be curious about the other students. However, to persevere on a day-to-day basis, you need more than curiosity. You have to cultivate from it the *desire* to become more involved. Otherwise you may not last to the end of your first year. Your initial investment of time and money will be lost. You may become like the student, Jerry, who endured four years of what he felt was drudgery merely for the sake of getting a degree. He graduated with little more than exhaustion, debts, and an aversion to further education. It would be easy to blame the large classrooms or the lack of individual attention. However, Jerry had more of a part in his boredom than he wants to admit.

Although the desire to learn may begin with curiosity, it is best fed by an open, eager, and flexible mind. Doug was a freshman who had planned out his entire college curriculum in his first semester. He had decided what classes he would take and what ones he would avoid based on his interests of the moment. He did not yet know all that was out there to learn, although he believed that he knew very well what he wanted to do. Then, in his sophomore year, he took a course that had borderline relevance to his goals. To his surprise, he became so enthused that he shot off in another direction altogether. By his junior year, he had developed yet a third direction and had completely lost track of his "system."

The desire to learn is the foundation to the desire to succeed. Wanting to *know* empowers you to do whatever is necessary. While you may be "just one" of several hundred students crammed into a massive classroom auditorium, you can retain your motivation while you are developing your long-range skills by giving yourself some initial success with several techniques: reinterpreting material, making yourself visible, using discipline, and recharging your interest.

1) *Reinterpret the material into your own frame of reference, and keep expanding it.* It is all too easy to dismiss a subject, especially in a required course, as being irrelevant to anything you want to do. However, a subject that seems irrelevant may actually be related to other subjects that do interest you. For example, knowledge and mastery of computers is intricately related to logic (usually offered in the philosophy department). Computer technology is also

touched by math, ethics, cognitive psychology, and the dynamics of learning a language. You may not see the connections unless you actively look for the value in the course. The will to learn is the discipline to search any subject for something that can weave into your primary concerns; it is also the will to allow your interests to expand into more directions and other fields. Additionally, it is the desire to go beyond a given subject and learn for the sheer joy of discovery.

Consider the story of Charles, told by psychologist Philip Barker. Charles' parents loved to walk on the beach each night to enjoy the ocean and the health benefits. Charles was uninterested in either, yet he had to accompany them because he was too young to stay at home by himself. He wandered along, looking at his feet. One day he noticed an unusual shell. He picked it up and took it to school to read about it in the library. The information was so interesting that he looked forward to the next walk on the beach to find more shells. He soon became more involved in the daily ritual than his parents were.

The story teaches us that there may be interesting things to learn even in classes we dislike if we keep our eyes open. You never know what you might discover.

Susan, a physical therapy major who was nearly finished with her program, attended a philosophy course just to find out what Socrates had said and whether it might have any impact on her thinking. She was interested in going beyond the curriculum that had been set up for her by her advisor, and she was able to find exciting connections that were not obvious to others. In contrast, Joe, a philosophy major, was interested only in what his favorite philosopher had to say. He paid attention to nothing else. For him, not only was the vast subject of philosophy closed off, but so was everything else in the college curriculum.

Your personal frame of reference can give useful context and meaning to new material, but be open to broadening it. Use your frame of reference but don't allow it to cut you off from opportunities.

2) *Make yourself visible to the professor.* Ask questions.

Attend office hours. Express your interest. Few professors will ignore sincere students. Dig for more information than the textbook or lecture yields. If you *really* want to know (as opposed to just wanting to impress the professor), you will increase both your scholastic and personal advantages. You are in that classroom for *your* sake. Keep your own priorities in mind.

3) *Use discipline as an aid.* It can help you to set priorities by keeping your goals in focus. Discipline is a negative word in our culture, but it does not have to be. You can change your attitude about it and allow it to become a positive part of your motivation by finding ways to see it as a means of gaining rewards.

4) *You must also learn the importance of recharging your interest.* Even the most enthusiastic student can get stale. Learn to keep a balance. Take a break from studying. Talk over your ideas with friends. Take the weekend and go to the beach or into the city or down the canyon or camping in the woods. Break routines. Read a detective novel. Sometimes the worst thing you can do for your enthusiasm is to overlearn. When your mouth is full of food to the point where you are no longer getting nourishment because you cannot chew, the thing to do is to take a break rather than to stuff more in.

In summary, the desire to learn is the development of curiosity, enthusiasm, discipline, balance, and the ability to stay open to new ideas and experiences. The first two will get you through the early stages of mastering the art, and the others will help to maintain learning as a productive lifetime habit. It is important that you take steps to motivate yourself as you move through the process involved in the art of inner learning.

It may be less frustrating if you view your approach to learning as you would to developing any new skill: as something you need for achieving a goal. As with other skills, learning involves steps and you can get through them more easily, and with less frustration, if you can turn the activity into a challenge, a means to an end.

A word about success, however: it is important to set

goals, and you will be more motivated if you believe that learning this process will help you to succeed with your goals, but you will do better if you focus on the process. In this case, success is like sleep. If you think about it too much or try to force it, it will surely elude you. If, however, you relax and allow it to happen as a result of bettering your skills, your chances are greater for achieving what you desire. That may seem to make little sense, but you will understand it better as we move along. Although I will mention success as a goal for which to strive, keep in mind that it is the process, itself, that should draw your primary attention.

_____ The Beginner's Mind

As I said before, it is difficult to be a beginner, and in some courses, you may experience the frustration and intimidation often associated with situations that call for skills you have not yet developed. Dr. Arnold Lazarus and Dr. Bernie Zilbergeld note in their research on techniques for better performance in any endeavor that two key factors are a receptive state and a positive framework in which to view your situation. You can develop the former by working on the latter.

Consider learning a new and complex game, like chess. First you have to know the rules. Reading through them can be like encountering a foreign language, but you persevere because you want to play a game. You forget the first rule by the time you get to the third, mostly because you have little context with which to make it meaningful. You usually have to read the rules several times, then refer back to them often as you play the game. There may be some frustration but you accept that as part of being a beginner and look forward to honing your skills until you achieve a greater sense of control and mastery.

It is in actually *playing* that you learn best, and if you play against someone who knows the game, you find out all too quickly that knowledge of the rules and the function of the pieces will rarely (if ever) win you the game. You must also develop strategies and learn to anticipate your opponent's moves. There is an *inner* game going on that transcends the mechanics.

The skill of learning can be similarly frustrating. As a new student, you feel awkward and out of place. You fumble around, trying to figure out how to balance your time, and how to make your mind retain information that seems foreign to you. You may or may not possess the security of past academic success, but even if you do, college is a different game altogether. You have no track record. To the professor, you are just another student. And unlike chess, the rules are not written out for you in a book. You may seek an advisor, but most advice will be general, and not necessarily comprehensible in a situation already overwhelming you with new experiences. Too much advice can be as detrimental as too little. You can become anxious and confused, perhaps homesick for family or friends. Developing the inner control that bears resemblance to the inner game of a chess master can give you a way to handle the confusion.

To get a sense of the stages of the process, think about the experience of learning to drive a car. For some people, the skill is quickly achieved. For others, however, it takes longer, with more frustration along the way, especially with a stick-shift car. The clutch must be mastered while trying to steer, and while remembering where the blinker controls are. If it is raining, you must think about lights and wind-shield wipers. At the same time, you must keep your speed under control, watch cars in the rearview mirror, and steer clear of other cars and pedestrians. There is an initial period where the machine seems foreign, and there are simply too many instructions to keep straight and remember while negotiating busy streets. As you pick up speed, you must forget everything else in an attempt to keep the car under control. However, as you grow used to it, you relax and enjoy it more. Your college experience can move along similar channels.

The first couple of days of orientation may seem to you

rather complex but certainly masterable. Beware! It will not be long before the pace picks up. Then you may find yourself trying to juggle all sorts of abstract instructions at the same time you are trying to learn the content of several courses. Exams will overtake you before you know it, sometimes within two or three weeks! You may be tempted to give up. That is the trap of the initial stages of being a beginner.

A freshman in a logic course became so frustrated with trying a learn formulas that made no sense to her that she became angry and depressed. She wanted to drop the course but she did not want to think of herself as having failed to grasp something that was supposed to be fairly basic. I urged her to think of another experience that had seemed confusing for her but that she had eventually mastered. She told me about learning how to use a computer. At first, there was so much to remember and nothing seemed to make sense. The commands were in code and there were more keys on the keyboard than there had been on her typewriter. She had made many mistakes and had believed that typing her papers to the keyboard and learned the commands, she realized that she had been wrong; using the computer was much more efficient, flexible, and even more fun than typing, and she was glad she had stuck with it. I told her to keep that experience in mind as she struggled with logic. The same thing could happen for her, once she grew used to working with a new tool. She stayed in the class and eventually the subject became easier for her. As long as she kept in mind that a process involved stages, she was able to stick with it and even to relax and allow herself to get used to it. The more she relaxed, the more easily she absorbed the material. Being depressed and angry only succeeded in hindering her ability to learn.

Before you continue, think about your own experience with a complex skill. Try to recall your initial frustration and your eventual achievement, then keep this experience in mind, like the logic student did with her computer mastery, as you move through this book.

An alternative is to view this stage of the college experience as a kind of *relationship,* like making a new friend. There may be moments of awkwardness. You may resist making an effort because you fear looking like a fool as you fumble around for something to say. You seek the familiarity of a kindred soul, but to achieve it, you have to go through the first uncomfortable stages of "breaking the ice." More often than not, your efforts will be rewarded, but the effort must be made in order to receive the reward.

The key is to keep reminding yourself that the early stages are going to be uncomfortable. Try not to blame yourself or become self-critical. You are not at fault. As Socrates says, the truly wise person knows that he does not know. That is the place to begin. Realize that there is a starting point for everything and find a way to "anchor" yourself in the process by remembering that learning to learn is like learning any other skill. Keep yourself actively involved in giving a context to this information in order to allow yourself to experience the first disconcerting stage as a necessary but *temporary* part of the process. Keep your goals in mind so that clumsiness is viewed not as *incompetence* but as merely the initial self-conscious gap between yourself and the tool. Work on reinterpreting the negative idea of "difficulty" as the postive idea of "challenge." Use past successes, academic or otherwise, to affirm that you have met and conquered challenges. View the uncertainty itself as a new challenge.

A common slogan of lottery games is, "you've got to be in it to win it." The same goes for the experience of learning in college. You have to allow it to make its claim on you, including the initial discomfort. As you get used to it (as with driving a car), what once seemed "too much to remember" can become automatic. The gap between you and the skill of learning begins to close.

Self-as-Instrument

Let's go back to the driving example. Initially, sitting in the driver's seat, looking at the steering wheel, the shift, the pedals, it felt awkward. When you focused on that tricky clutch, you forgot to put on your blinkers to signal to turn. Or while you watched behind to back your car into a parking space, you forgot to watch for the curb and ended up hitting it (or another car). But soon, the nervousness and self-consciousness decreased as your mastery increased. Now you drive without thinking about gear shifts and clutches and blinker lights. You have absorbed the skill into your subconscious, where it stays, unless something like a malfunction in the brakes or mishandling of the shift brings the action to your awareness. For the most part, the skill has become a function of the mind absorbed into the body. It is you, yourself, who are the instrument rather than the steering wheel. You are the *center*. The achievement of this state of skill is the result of technical mastery and of a merging of your own consciousness with whatever it is you are focusing on. Understanding this is the second step, after motivation, toward the *inner* experience of learning.

Take the simpler example of using a typewriter, something that all students must (or should) learn. At first the layout of the keys seems confusing and illogical. It seems extremely unnatural not to look at each key as your finger hits it. But with more practice, you get used to the layout, and soon your fingers become indistinguishable from the keys. It is you who are typing, not the machine. The gap between you and the machine has closed and you are now the instrument. You have *grown into* the skill to the point where you have taken it on as part of yourself.

Mastering skills involves transforming something external and foreign to something internal and intimately connected to you. An analogy would be the difference between observing someone running a computer program and actually running it yourself. You see through different eyes when the keyboard is under your fingers. The *experience* of running a computer program has a different quality than simply listening to someone offer an explanation. Because you feel more *connected* to the experience, it becomes less of an external object. Therefore the more you participate, the more it becomes part of you.

The same idea holds true in the classroom. Gathering facts without personal involvement and connection is like trying to hold grains of sand in your hand. At first, it will seem that you have quite a handful, but eventually most of it will slip away. You may then think that all you need is some sort of container, but what good will it do you to have all that sand sitting around in a container? For the sand to be useful to you, you need to have some purpose in mind, a context that gives it *meaning* and a way to make it *experientially* real to you. The rest of this book will assist you in that regard.

_____ Summary

Professors, subjects, or college settings, do not define learning, rather learning is an extension of life. You can learn no matter where you are. Education neither starts nor stops at the doors of a college or university. Developing a positive and motivating approach to the process of learning will not only help you through your college years, but through post-college careers, and even throughout your life.

The skill of learning, like most skills, involves a period of clumsiness and intimidation while you get used to it. With practice, and motivated by the desire to learn, you will soon close the gap between yourself and the process of learning until you *become* a learner using your mind and body as the primary instruments. Understanding this will move you toward the kind of mastery that is achieved with inner resources.

You will enjoy your education more and you will reap more long-term benefits if you find ways to be involved in it. Experts on peak performance around the world attest to the fact that striving for inner control and satisfaction makes success more likely than striving for success, itself. Achieving success as a result of simply enjoying what you are doing will make you feel good, and feeling good will make you continue to enjoy learning.

Exercises ———————————————————————————

Before you go on to the next chapter, you will gain some advantage in understanding how the art of inner learning can benefit you if you first take time to assess your own learning style. Attend to each of the following items and describe your approach. From the list, try to assess your motivating values. Try to be as specific as possible. Keep your description to look at when you finish the book:

1. Studying
2. Reading
3. Asking questions
4. Taking notes
5. Organizing notes
6. Making important decisions
7. Approaching important tasks
8. Approaching tasks you dislike

9. Solving problems
10. Planning your future
11. Setting goals
12. Working with others
13. Dealing with stress
14. Asking for help
15. Discussions
16. Dealing with setbacks

2

Learning As Partners

I once polled a class about what they felt most affected their learning. The majority focused blame or praise on the professor. I wanted them to become more actively involved in their education rather than relying on me. Yet they resisted my efforts to get them to become more independent and to learn to teach themselves. That was *not*, they insisted, "the way" it was done!

I think the sudden responsibility frightened them. They were used to the teacher being central and had developed a set of expectations about how a class was to be run. For them, that was the only way to learn. Anything new confused them. *Their* job, they felt, was to wait passively, ready to sponge up the flow of data which I, as professor, should give to them. Only when they eventually gave up these expectations and began to experience the energy and pleasure of *active* participation did they become enthused. However, the habits were not easy for them to break and required that they take a look at themselves to see how they had developed the mindset that had trapped them into passivity in the first place. That attitude and its opposite is the focus of this chapter.

Students tend to believe, falsely, that their minds are blank slates that the teacher must fill with information. Because the teacher supposedly knows what they do not, it is his or her responsibility to deliver information clearly so that they can add it to their storage of facts or abilities. Such a view is a misunderstanding of the relationship that should develop between teachers and their students.

The attitude is often blamed on the educational system. There is some truth in this. Certainly both students and teachers participate in maintaining the lecture/note-taking format that is most popular in the classroom. It is easier and carries less risk for both parties. It also gives the teacher more control. However, recent research has shown this method to have no more educational benefit than if students were to read the information for themselves in textbooks. Unfortunately, with regard to changing this practice, a vicious cycle is created because adopting this passive style as a tradition discourages creative teaching that might involve the students more actively in the classroom—to the greater enjoyment of everyone, including the teacher.

Your personal attitude toward learning is in *your* hands. If you truly want to get the most out of your college education, you must resist the pressures of tradition and try a new path. The road to every kind of success is paved with independent, creative thinking—an essential component of the art of inner learning. You will only learn how to develop this if you understand from the start that you must take a more active interest in your education than you are used to.

The Learning Tradition

In the brochure of a leadership program, a claim was made that if we are to produce leaders from the college-age population, learning environments must change. Students must be encouraged to participate. They must be encouraged to create thoughtful responses of their own, to become involved in outside activities that could deepen their intellectual grasp of the material. Sounds wonderful on paper. Yet, in the classroom, it's easier said than done.

Unfortunately, the traditional expectations are the result of many years of training, and strong psychological barriers maintain the status quo. From the lowest grades, the class *sits and listens* as the teacher *says*. Deviation risks suspicion. When someone wants to try something new, others may read into their act an implicit criticism of the old way of doing things. That includes criticizing the people who practice it. So they resist and try to keep change from happening. There is also some fear that if the new approach works, they will be forced to try it and they may be unwilling to put themselves on the line. This happened in one school system, and those who could not adapt had to quit. In addition, teachers may feel it is their duty to protect students from the confusion that can result with trying something new.

However, confusion is not necessarily negative. Wonderful new discoveries can emerge from shaking up old systems. The entire history of science bears witness to this. There may be some discomfort at the lack of security, and confusion has the capacity to paralyze, yet it cannot be denied that change can have a positive effect. In the movie, *Hoosiers,* a basketball coach introduces a small-town team to a new way of playing basketball which involves unfamiliar methods. The team is asked to give up former rituals in favor of a more basic and disciplined routine. The old coach resists this in an attempt to protect the boys from getting confused and playing badly and at first, they *do* play badly. They resent their new coach for forcing them to feel so awkward when they cannot follow his instructions very well. Yet as they get used to the new system, relax and concentrate on playing, the more team-oriented, fundamental approach makes a much better team than they ever had been with the old system.

It requires an act of faith to try something new. Many teachers have expressed fear that the students will not respond, and their fear may be justified. You, as a student, want to be assured of the results before you take any risks. If someone offered you food which you had never seen before and assured you that it was nutritionally wholesome, you would not have to trust that person unless you were in great need of the food. Your physical hunger would guide you in taking a risk. Unfortunately, unlike the situation with your body, you can be starving intellectually without realizing it, and you cannot judge easily whether the risk is worthwhile.

In a classroom situation where there is so much concern about grades and structure, students are rarely willing to try a new approach. Learning something new makes them vulnerable. They are used to the traditional way of getting the grade they want. They know what is required of them and they know how to make the system work for them. A new approach threatens them with possible failure, or with less clearly measurable success than that offered under traditional systems.

Robert M. Pirsig, the college professor who wrote *Zen and the Art of Motorcycle Maintanence,* experienced this. He wanted to spend the semester teaching without the feedback of grades, in order to encourage his students to develop the more vague notion of "quality" in their work. They strongly objected, despite his belief that they would do better work and enjoy it more if they were not concentrating on a structured grading system. The students, however, could not see that their past educational training had *created* their perceptions of the situation. They believed that the tradition was the only way to operate in college because that is what they had been taught. They did not understand that context and attitudes determine perception and that changing the *situation* could change their *perception.* They did not realize that there were more ways to participate in the learning process than the one they knew, primarily because the context in which they had been taught was formed by a system that tends, for the sake of simplicity and manageability, *not* to acknowledge alternative visions.

Yet it cannot be denied that almost any situation can be interpreted in more than one way. A woman walked into an empty auditorium and saw a man in the orchestra pit on the conductor's platform. He was waving his hands about in the silent room with his eyes closed. When he saw the woman, he invited her in to "listen to the music." Realizing that as a trained conductor he had skills and visions beyond anything she could exercise, she surrendered her imagination as he vividly described the

sound of the trombones, the kettle drums, the flutes. Soon
it seemed to her that she could hear it for herself. She was
impressed and made a note to return for this conductor's
performance. Just then another man entered and called
out that it was time to sweep in front of the building. The
woman suddenly realized that the "conductor" was a
janitor. Had she known of his position before she "listened
to the music," she might have thought him only a foolish
old man. Instead, the frame of reference had allowed her
to believe enough in him to "hear" the music. How she
saw the man influenced her experience. Our own beliefs
do the same for us (and to us) each day.

For example, if you were told by a friend that Professor
Smith was "tough" and that's why he was an excellent
teacher, you might approach his assignments more positively than if that same friend had told you he was a
teacher to avoid because he was "tough." Thus, a "tough"
professor can be perceived as both excellent and terrible
for the exact same assignments from different points of
view, and it is your point of view that will influence your
classroom experience.

One of the key factors in getting yourself actively involved in your education is the ability to acknowledge that
there are many contexts of interpretation for any classroom
situation. How you approach your own education will
affect the choices you make.

Think of your mind as an artist's canvas. Not a blank
canvas, necessarily, but one on which you can change
detail. You must decide on how this picture will turn out.
You can take one of three directions: 1) only *you* will
paint what goes on the canvas, 2) only the teacher will
decide what the picture will be, or 3) you and the teacher
will work together. (You should see from these options
that even the choice to be passive and let another do the
work is a choice that *you* make!)

If you choose the first option, you will be sealed into
your own mind, and you will learn little or nothing. The
second option deprives you of control and allows you only

a superficial sense of what the other person is painting. The third option, however, gives you the best of both: the opportunity to learn from someone who may know more, but also a sense of control and a better grasp of what you are learning.

Learning is a partnership. How well the partnership works is a function of both participants. You cannot be responsible for how well your teachers keep up their end, but you are responsible for yourself. There are strategies available for maximizing your skills and opportunities for learning in spite of what is presented in the classroom. How well the strategies will work will depend on your attitude and motivation.

 Passive Attitudes

A psychology professor once asked a classroom of students to write down the difference between a passive and an active approach to education. The majority expressed a very simplistic idea of the passive approach as one of inactivity: "The passive person says nothing and thinks about nothing." Students who believe that are in danger of becoming passive without realizing it.

Passivity is akin to what psychologist Ellen J. Langer calls "mindlessness" or living our lives "on automatic." Information is processed in a narrow and rigid manner without thoughtful evaluation. We accept everything at face value. It is like the person who asks, "how are you?" and does not hear your answer because it was a routine greeting that had no real meaning.

"Mindfulness," on the other hand, is attention to the present moment that involves an openness to experience and an ability to transcend rigid mindsets. Mindful people think about what they do and say, and are aware of how they create their own perspectives. To participate fully in life, says Dr. Langer, one must do so *mindfully*, becoming aware of your range of options and more aware of the manner in which you participate in a given situation.

Our minds are not naturally passive. As a child, you were probably curious, constantly seeking and discovering. You asked questions and went off in many directions, depending on what sparked your interest from moment to moment. You were constantly surprised and thrilled, and you probably irritated adults with your endless probing. Soon your behavior and mind were channeled into directed activities by parents and teachers who wanted you to learn in a more focused and disciplined manner. In the typical scenario, you were taught what to think and say, how to behave and which words and mannerisms were inappropriate. You were expected to obey, and deviations were either discouraged or punished. Although not all schools take this approach, and some even recognize the problem with it, for many schools, it becomes the easiest way to manage students. According to education expert Ronald Gross in *Peak Learning,* traditional learning approaches emphasize memorization and repetition, linear intellectual development, conformity, static processes, and teachers as information providers.

As you developed focus, you may have learned how to be passive. Your teachers had a lot of information to pour into your mind, and you were to sit and be filled, with the emphasis on memorization and "right" answers. Little may have been done to encourage independent thinking. If you learned to be passive, however, you also learned how to be bored. With boredom, your mind gradually gives up its differentiating function and you may begin to rely on superficial processing in order to comprehend the flow of incoming data. Your passive stance may then have been reinforced as a defense against the anxiety of not doing well according to the expectations of others. Soon you may have started looking to your mother or father to decide for you what you should do that day. As a result, you began to lose the spontaneous art of thinking up for yourself some stimulating activity. Your increasingly more focused attention span became a silent tapeworm on your earlier, more expansive enjoyment of learning, and you grew used to having others tell you what to do and how to think. Although this scenario was not necessarily inevitable, the most traditional educational programs that emphasize information and neglect independent thinking make it more likely than not that you were caught up in such a cycle.

Before you knew it, you were sitting at a desk for increasingly more hours per day. Competition set in and you were forced to "sink or swim"—to adapt yourself to this passive learning style in a way that outdistanced other students. Memorization, taking notes verbatim, and reproducing material on tests probably became the dominant focus of your learning efforts, and you came to equate these activities with learning. They may have stood you in good stead through high school, and could continue to do so in college, but such practices are structured, cued into the classroom, and are not very adaptive to post-college careers. Compare your own experience with that of Carolyn's below.

Carolyn had a college professor who believed firmly in these principles of learning. He was teaching a psychology course on learning theories and engaged in continuous verbal battle with Carolyn over what she was actually getting out of the class. She insisted that memorization was not only not sufficient, but not necessary, since she could always go find the information. When she consistently scored high on every test, he would say with great exasperation: "Can you still say you are not learning?"

He expected that she would not disregard her own "success." Her answer to him, however, was that she had simply memorized well. She had good short-term memory. She was "successful" as a product of the system, but not satisfied. Ask her today what she got out of that class and she cannot recall any of the facts or formulas. All she remembers is how she struggled to understand why memorizing names, definitions, and theories that she could easily find in a book if she ever needed them, left her feeling hollow and bored. Her experience is not unusual.

Learning is not just content, but involves skills in making the material meaningful and applicable to your concerns. We cannot learn when we are bored. We cannot learn when we have no opportunity to take the material through serious reflections for examining its value for ourselves. Boredom and mindless memorization are inherent in the passive style of learning.

You may think you know exactly what to do to change from passive to active. You probably have a mental picture of what the passive style is like: a person slumped in a chair, half-daydreaming, taking notes, hearing but not listening. While you would be correct in thinking that just to sit up and start concentrating would diminish some of the negative side-effects of passive performance, you may not realize that there is much more to making the change than correcting your posture and asking a few questions. Active learning is the result of an inner attitude change; taking care of external appearances with resolutions that you set for yourself will last about as long as a New Year's resolution.

Before I describe the attitude that might serve you best, take a look at various classroom styles that may be construed as "active," but are really a disguise for a passive mind. Recognizing them for what they are can keep you from adopting them as a means of changing your old habits. It is not the *event* of changing your habits but *what* you change them *to* that counts.

The Chameleon

Joe tries to learn as much as he can. He moves from one professor to another and drinks in everything he hears. What he hears, he believes. He is a sponge. And like a sponge, he makes no discriminations. He takes in two sides of a controversial issue and fails to see the contradiction of believing both. He changes "color" to conform to whatever he hears. His activity may take a lot of time and effort, but it is essentially mindless; he is not *involved* as an independent thinker.

The Antagonist

Jerry likes to react to everything he hears. No matter what the teacher says, he resists, throwing comments back as if aiming darts at a dart board. His mind is like a ping-pong paddle. He has no time to reflect over anything he hears because he is too busy formulating his attack. Yet he depends on the teacher to give him what he needs before he can attack. He has no capacity for thinking for himself. He is aggressive but still passive because he reacts for the *sake* of reacting rather than *thinking about* what he is reacting to—and whether it really deserves a reaction.

_____ The Adjudicator

Nancy likes to consider both sides of everything. Whenever she is faced with taking a position, she carefully states the merits and demerits of each side of the issue. She never gets around to taking her own stand because she knows only how to accumulate and convey all the information, not how to make decisions about it.

_____ The Competent

Diane appears to know exactly what she is doing. She gets the highest scores on every exam, and is always prepared to refer to the textbook. She retains well and memorizes well. Yet she cannot think for herself. She is a mirror. She can reflect back what comes to her, but she can generate nothing on her own.

_____ The Indecisive

Mark listens to everything but cannot make up his mind about any of it. He simply never knows whether to respond or react, to agree or disagree. Everything floats through his head, "in one ear and out the other," because he has no grasp of how to anchor the information through personal reflection and decision.

_____ The Scrambler

Moreen listens attentively, but clutters anything she hears with her own thoughts before she has a chance to really listen to what is being said. As a consequence, she asks many questions which have already been clarified or which are beside the point of the material. Her questions confuse others in the class, and even when she receives answers, she scrambles them and still fails to understand the material. She takes up much class time but yields little of value.

Because there is some sort of activity involved, the student believes he or she is an active learner. However, *activity* is not equivalent to a genuinely active *attitude*. The examples are clear illustrations of Langer's notion of "mindlessness." The students adopt routines and fail to really think about what they are doing. They trap themselves into a "learned" mindset, and strain their experience through restrictive attitudes. The routines yield a sense of security that actually *prevents* them from developing an active approach, and ultimately inhibits them from learning anything.

An *active* approach to learning would involve the ability to think through what you are doing, to transcend your mindset, and to engage yourself as fully as possible in the present moment of any event, such as a lecture in a classroom. While there may be as many active *styles* as there are passive styles, they are not as deceptive. The basics of the active approach can be developed by following through on the suggestions set out in the chapters of this book.

To get out of a passive style, students need to become more aware of themselves, their environment, and their learning opportunities, and to care about them.

_____ Becoming Aware

Think about a noise in your environment that you have grown used to, for example, an air conditioner or heater. You no longer attend to it, yet it still seeps into the fringes of your consciousness. If you are tired, the noise may aggravate your irritation without becoming apparent to you as the cause. That is the way that mindlessness works. We remain unaware of aspects of our situations, closing them off with routine ways of thinking and perceiving. We thus have little control over their effect on us.

Now think of a time when you heard a noise that you were unable to identify. You forgot everything else as you focused your attention on identifying the sound (especially if you were alone at night). The longer the sound remained a mystery, the more your hearing sharpened until you almost seemed to become nothing but an ear. These two experiences illustrate the difference between passive mindlessness and active, mindful attention.

It is important for you to assess your own degree and style of awareness, and to decide whether you need to consider making a change. Look over the exercise you did at the end of the last chapter. How much of what you do leans toward a passive style, and how much is active, alert and involved? You can learn more about how to become aware of your style through exercises in focus and imagery, offered in later chapters, but first you must become more *self* aware, and that requires a different type of process, covered in an upcoming chapter. Prior to self-awareness, you must be able to recognize the goal.

 The Active Mind

Learning occurs in a field of motion. Language appears and disappears quickly. A stagnant, tired or undisciplined mind will grasp only the minimal message, if it grasps anything at all. There was a popular joke about a teacher who suggested to her students that they might learn more if they did not try to take notes verbatim. One student raised his hand and asked, "How do you spell 'verbatim'?" That was a "mindless" response.

Students too often attempt to transcribe a lecture verbatim, and this activity mirrors their entire approach to their classroom behavior. However, it is a futile exercise.

The words come to them as *noncontextual units,* rather than grouped as whole thoughts. They often miss much of what is being said because they have adopted the attitude of passive recorders. They are not *listening* to the lecture, and they cannot possibly record every word, so chances are that they miss important items. Only with an active mind comes the clarity and comprehension that grasps whole, intelligible thoughts. *Really listening* means giving up the practice of trying to write down everything that is said and adopting an approach that *comprehends* in the moment and is able to focus on the items of true significance.

The active mind is akin to that of an unrepressed child. It is curious, spontaneous, alert, open, resonant. You must try to recapture that searching, probing, uncluttered intensity that you once possessed, and learn to channel it through a form of discipline that does not encourage passivity. Good learning and poor learning are the result of perceptions and habits which can be changed. The learner will decide the quality, no one else. Section Two provides you with ways to develop these skills.

The active mind is also aware of its ignorance. Too often, ignorance is viewed with suspicion and avoided. However, it is a crucial ingredient to the learning process. We are motivated to replace ignorance with knowledge only if we *realize* we are ignorant. The philosopher, Socrates, was famous for his approach to learning about difficult concepts, such as courage and love. He adopted the posture of ignorance, imploring those who seemed to "know" to bestow on him their knowledge. He questioned their blithe, superficial definitions and ideas to the point where they either left in a huff or admitted that perhaps they did not know as much as they thought. Their "knowledge" had blinded them to their ignorance and to genuine opportunities to learn, whereas Socrates' ignorance had moved him continually to probe for clarity.

Recognizing our own true ignorance helps to erode the stumbling block of conceit or fear. Often when we think we know something, or when we are afraid to admit we may not, our minds shut out new information or new approaches that might actually be superior to those that we currently utilize.

To adopt an attitude of ignorance does not mean to view your mind as a "tabula rasa"—or blank slate. It means to realize that by the time you get to college, you have a great deal of information to sort through, as well as many experiences. But if you enter with the belief that you already "know," why go at all? Stan "knew" so much that he never listened. Instead, everything the professor said was filtered through his "knowledge" to the point where it was distorted. It became clear that his "knowledge" was the result of a previous class that had touched superficially on the subject and that was as much as he knew about it. His weakness was that he *believed* that he knew more than he did. He left the class "knowing" as little as when he came in.

Ignorance helps you to be willing to learn. Willingness to learn unblocks energy. You can *feel* the difference. Think about coming into your first class of the day with a passive attitude. You slump into the chair and sit there, your mind in a state of nothingness, until the professor enters. You don't move until she starts to lecture. Then you begrudgingly open your notebook and begin to take notes. You are already several minutes behind. Your mind churns to keep up and it clutters your efforts with the echo of what is being said *now*. You think the clock must have stopped. You can't wait for class to be over. The entire experience is an unpleasant effort and you feel exhausted when it is finally time to leave. If you enter with a passive, "know-it-all" attitude, your boredom and irritation only increase.

Now imagine (or remember) going into the class eager for the experience and open to the possibility that there are things you don't know and want to know. You sit up in your seat. You feel good. You are alert and ready to become involved. The atmosphere is charged and you are enjoying it. You feel alive, open, perhaps even creative. Time seems to fly! You are surprised when the professor ends the class, and you feel energized and awake, excited about thinking over what you have heard or written. If this has ever happened to you, then you have an advantage in putting an active approach into place as a permanent foundation to your college experience because you have experienced some of the rewarding results.

It may surprise you to hear that *both* of these experiences are possible in the *same* classroom. Why? Because the style of learning is a result of the attitude you adopt, and that gets us back to the heart of this chapter—that the responsibility for your approach is your part of the educational partnership.

_____ The Learning Partnership

Your professor is typically a person who is somewhere ahead of you on the path to knowledge and wisdom. College professors possess a wide variety of styles and degrees of skill. You may not like one teacher's style, but he or she may still have something to offer. Give your teachers the benefit of the doubt. They are in the position for a reason. Get to know them. Let them get to know you. Even in a class of three or four hundred students, make yourself known (though not obnoxiously so). Visit the professor's office hours. Then, when you prepare or write a paper or take a test, you have a relationship on the line. You want respect and recognition. Only if the professor knows you can he or she encourage you or recognize that you are making an effort.

You can facilitate your learning by recognizing and maximizing the partnership. Or you can harm your progress by ignoring it. Such a relationship will often motivate you to do your best and to be prepared, if only to avoid the embarrassment of becoming conspicuous through failure or neglect.

There are a variety of partnership styles, not all of which are appropriate to the student/teacher relationship:

1. An *agency* relationship gives all the authority and responsibility for making decisions to the student. The teacher acts under the student's direction.

2. A *contract* relationship is where authority and responsibility are shared equally.

3. A *friendship* is personal, involving mutual interests and activities.

4. A *paternalistic* partnership puts the professor in authority over the student as the one who decides what is best, and takes full responsibility, as a parent to a child.

5. In partnerships based on *fiduciary* arrangements, the professor's expertise is recognized, but students retain some degree of responsibility for the benefits they derive from the relationship. The teacher is a guide of sorts, even a midwife, helping you to get in touch with your own talents and potential, mostly helping you to learn to teach yourself.

The teacher/student relationship is best defined as a fiduciary relationship. Each person recognizes the other's talents and role. It is not a friendship where you are on equal footing with one another, nor is it to be characterized as paternalism, where the teacher watches over you. Never confuse getting to know the professor with the guarantee of getting a good grade because you are friendly. In a fiduciary relationship, one partner is in a superior position by virtue of knowledge, skill or expertise, but the best teacher, according to a Zen proverb, is one who teaches you how to get the food yourself. Both participants in the relationship have a responsibility, and for the partnership to work, both must take their responsibility seriously. If your professor is not facilitating the relationship, the worst thing to do is to simply give up and give in. You may motivate him or her to become a better teacher by being a better student.

_____ Summary

The active and passive attitude require a "survival of the fittest" approach. Like two dogs fighting, the strongest one will win. And this will be the one you feed. If you feed your passive mind, you will get a dog who only feeds off you. If you feed the active mind, you will get a dog who will return your efforts and eventually benefit you.

Just *wanting* to learn, however, is rarely sufficient. You have acquired many traits along the way in your education and personality development that may hinder you in your pursuit. It is important that you examine the potential interferences. Knowing your values and that there are other options can give you the mobility to learn from various teaching styles. Some will instantly resonate for you, and these will help to smooth the learning process. Those teaching styles that have less appeal will encourage you to question and transcend your disatisfaction with little effort.

In the following chapter, I describe your responsibility in being prepared, but it does not end there. You will also have to examine your own capacity to *become* an active learner. It will be more difficult for some than for others, but anyone can eventually master the process of inner learning and reap a lifetime of rewards.

Exercise _____

Think about an assignment you have received in class. View it positively and describe your feelings about completing it.

Now view it in a negative light and compare those feelings to your positive perspective. What did you learn?

Think about how perspective can affect the quality of learning in the relationship you develop with your teachers in the classroom, and write down all the possibilities you can imagine.

Do the same exercises from a passive and an active perspective.

3

Being Prepared

Larry had to make a decision, after receiving an unfair grade on a paper he had worked hard on. He felt the professor had misunderstood what he had been trying to say, and debated with himself about going to talk to her. He had heard that she was hard-nosed about her grading and assumed he would receive no special consideration. After fuming about it, he finally approached the professor after class one day. To his surprise, she invited him back to her office to discuss it. He was completely unprepared for this response and stumbled through his defense. Although the professor seemed inclined to raise his grade if he could offer a good reason, Larry was unable to discuss his ideas clearly enough to convince her, and was too embarassed to ask for another chance.

Most people have experienced similar frustrations at lost opportunities that rested on their own preparation. Try to recall a situation in which you were unprepared and remember the feelings you had. Chances are, this is a situation you would have avoided if you could have.

The same kind of thing can occur in many other aspects of college life (and later, in the career for which the classroom is preparing you). Sometimes you cannot help being unprepared, but many times you can. Before you begin the steps involved in developing an attitude of active participation in your education, you must understand that skills are only useful if you are prepared to exercise them.

_____ Levels of Preparation

The responsibility of the student in the partnership of learning involves several levels of preparation: mechanical, emotional, and mental.

Mechanical preparedness

Mechanical preparedness, the most obvious form of preparation, involves having the time, place, and equipment necessary for optimum classroom performance. Too often, however, mechanical preparedness is equated with sufficient preparation. That is how the art of being a student gets lost.

Aside from the necessary pen or pencil, paper, and textbook, the actual physical needs are peculiar to the course requirements. If, for example, you have a Statistics or Engineering course, you will need a calculator. Similarly, if you have a dance class, you will need appropriate clothing. Art courses require a wide variety of materials.

However, simply having what you need does not necessarily mean that you are ready to learn. Sometimes when I come into class and begin a lecture, I find that students are scrambling to open their notebooks, to find a pen, to grab the right text (if they even have it with them). Unprepared students will miss the first minutes of the lecture because they were not ready to begin taking notes. I have to repeat things for them, to the detriment of the flow of my lecture, and often to the distraction and irritation of the other students.

Additional important factors include knowing the time and place, and being punctual to class or lab. I have had students show up a week late, two weeks late, even six weeks into the course. It is difficult to make up work that you miss, especially in the form of lectures. I have had students who assume I'll just hand over my notes, which is not a very wise assumption to make. To maximize your learning, figure out your schedule well ahead of the first day of class. Go to the building if it will help you get a sense of where you must go. And above all, do not come late into the classroom.

Many schools establish a set period of time, ten to twenty minutes, between classes for students to make it from one classroon to another. At one university where I taught, there are several campuses. Often students try to fit all their courses into the least possible amount of time, and typically end up having to cover several miles in that twenty-minute slot. Very few can accomplish it. The result is that students either leave early or sit restlessly at the edge of their seats waiting for one class to wind up, and the next to begin. They believe this practice has no effect on their learning. And it doesn't—if they believe that "learning" involves only cramming notes into a notebook.

What many students fail to understand is that leaving early and arriving late are disruptive, not just to the continuity of their own studies, but to the professor and other students in the room. To watch the clock in preparation for your "flight" takes your mind off the class and contributes to an atmosphere of restlessness that pulls other eyes to the clock. Even in an auditorium where three hundred students may be seated, the early departures and late entrances are noticed. In Part Three, I will describe the classroom as an organic system. I will also describe how to maximize the individual experience of learning. You will understand better why it is important to arrange your schedule in a way that creates the least disturbance to yourself and others.

One more aspect of being mechanically prepared is to do your assigned homework. The professor will typically organize the schedule so that, if it is followed, you will be able to balance the assignments. This method is not just for your benefit. The professor will expect you to follow through and do the assignments in order to coordinate with the classroom situation. If you read the assigned pages of text, then you will more clearly understand the lecture, or if you don't understand, you will at least have a grasp of the appropriate questions to ask. You will contribute more to a discussion, and you will benefit from others' discussion of the assigned reading.

If you fail to read what is expected, you will soon become buried with more assignments, and when it simply becomes too much for you to do, you may become frustrated and withdrawn. Students expect to "cram" but there is no reason why you have to adopt such an expectation or habit for yourself. It provides little benefit and results in a great deal of stress.

Writing is even more demanding. If you fail to get assignments in on time, there is often a penalty. Even when there is no explicit grade penalty, you will have the unfinished assignment hanging over your head, while more assignments continue to demand your time. If you trail behind, you will be picking up the crumbs rather than enjoying fresh bread. Many students decide that taking an "incomplete" is the catch-all to their neglect. However, time does not just stand still. There will be demands in your future that you cannot yet envision.

One person I know has created a fantasy for herself that she calls the "thirteenth month." She perceives this month as a time when she will catch up on all of her demands from the previous year. Although it is only a fantasy that she would like to imagine could come true, the idea of it encourages her to put things off. She never does get anything done.

Everyone would like an extra day, week, or even month to "catch-up," but they rarely get it. During a semester break or the summer, you have more demands and the work often gets pushed back. By the time you get to it, you will have lost the benefit of the classroom lectures to help you to understand the material. You may have to read the text and the lecture notes all over again, wasting more time. Or you may have to give up on the course, in which case, you've wasted even more of your time. Few people believe this will actually happen to them, yet I encounter students every year who flunk a course they had every intention of passing, merely because they could not get the work done.

To be prepared, you need to learn to set goals. While your principal goal may be to get a degree, you can best achieve this major goal by clarifying your objectives and setting minor goals along the way. The pressures of college usually require *daily* goals. You have four or five courses, each meeting one to three times per week, and each requiring effort on your part. Coordination becomes a way of life, but coordination must be combined with discipline.

Mental preparedness

Discipline is a way of using boundaries to gain the most freedom. This was mentioned earlier as a way to maintain your motivation, but it also assists you in increasing your level of mental preparation. You consciously and willingly choose to restrict your choices. That sounds contradictory, but imagine a river. It flows freely, and yet it does so only by virtue of the way it is channeled by its banks. Narrow the banks and the water power in the river is intensified.

Similarly, discipline, often confused with "burden," is simply a daily practice through which you deny yourself one thing in order to get another. In this way it is a form of freedom. At first it will be an effort. You may feel pressured, but it will eventually become as automatic as driving a car. The joy of eventual excellence and achievement will reinforce your new habits. Discipline brings the long-term, lasting gain over the short-term, transient gain, and you will have more freedom to do what you really want to do.

Consider for instance that you have an exam Friday morning, and your friends want you to go with them for pizza or to a party. You want to go with your friends (short-term pleasure), but you also want to do well on the exam (long-term benefits). The disciplined person can make the best choice: he or she will say "no" to whims that interfere with his or her true goals. As those goals are achieved, the discipline will seem less an effort than a means of exercising choice and control in your life.

The discipline of goal-setting involves both ultimate goals and process goals. If you enter college with no goals at all, you will become like a ship in a storm, tossed about by winds from all directions. If your goals are too vague, you will have no idea how to achieve them (or that you have achieved them). It is important, then, to *have* goals that are clear to you.

First you must figure out what it is you really want. If you are reading this book, I assume that what you really want is, at least, to do well in college. To do well might simply mean to achieve a certain gradepoint average. Such a goal is a process goal. A gradepoint average is a means to some end: a good feeling, better leverage for graduate school, a better grasp of some subject area. Be careful to make the distinctions. This book focuses on *process* goals, although I encourage you to set your long-term ultimate goal. Decide why you are at college and what you want to get out of your effort. Then decide what it will take to get what you want. Keep in mind that setting the goal does not mean becoming focused on it but rather to allow it to give direction to the choices you make.

Set goals each week, or even each day, if that will help keep your purpose clear to you. Write them down. Check to see if you have done what you set out to do, and reward yourself if you have. Even small victories need to be celebrated. Learn what you have done wrong if you haven't accomplished what you want, and make the appropriate changes. Don't allow setbacks to become major hurdles. Keep your ultimate goals in mind as a guideline and keep checking your progress. The more you say "no" to things that interfere with your goals, the stronger will be your vision and affirmation of your goals. Soon your discipline will become more habit and less effort, and the benefits of achieving what you want to achieve will become evident. Discipline is a crucial ingredient in being prepared for success in college. Don't become a stagnant pond. Keep the flow going.

Emotional preparedness

Often students associate college with freedom. No longer are their parents aware of what they are doing, what hours they keep, what friends they see. It is exhilaration! And yet unbridled freedom is less *genuine* freedom than is a disciplined freedom. Having no bounds, no standards, and no limits only becomes the kind of chaos and confusion that yields little benefit.

One student wanted to test the limits. He imposed none on himself, and none were imposed on him. He partied, he drank, he ignored his studies and his health, until one day he went too far. Still looking for limits to test, he got drunk at a sporting event and walked off the top seat of the bleachers. He was paralyzed from the neck down. Had you asked him before this happened, he would have said that he'd had no intention of risking his life or of crippling himself. Yet he did.

Less dramatic but just as important are students who simply fail to make it through college because they cannot set priorities and limits. It is important that you understand the value of limits and begin to set some for yourself. If *you* choose them, then you have more self-control than someone who forces circumstances to set them.

There are many opportunities to harm yourself at college. Drugs, alcohol, bad food, continuous parties, and poor study habits that result in "all-nighters" can become weapons against your health, against your will to learn, and against your future. What you do (or fail to do in college) will affect you most of the rest of your life. Flunking one exam may seem minor at first, until it brings down your grade, which in turn reduces your gradepoint average. If the course is in your major area of concentration, you may hurt your chances for a job or for getting into a good graduate program.

Sometimes students imagine they can make mistakes and get away with it by talking a professor into giving them grades they do not deserve. Sometimes it works. But it will not work with all professors, nor necessarily with the same one twice. Even with room to maneuver, you are not excused from eventually taking responsibility for yourself. Your parents are no longer there to guide or protect you. The assumption in college is that you will develop the maturity necessary to make the most of the opportunities offered.

To be emotionally prepared means to know yourself. In Chapter 7, I describe a technique for getting to know yourself better. In Chapter 4, I list many of the psychological traits common to students which can hinder your goals and performance, and following that, I list the traits that can facilitate it. Getting to know yourself becomes the stepping stone to doing something with what you discover. It is essential that you decide what you want to do with your education, whether that means you come to view education as a means toward a career or an end in itself. Only by developing all three levels of preparation will you gain the surest access to your inner resources.

There will be pressures on all sides to really "let loose," or to "have fun." You *should* have fun. But you should also know when "having fun" becomes an escape, an obsession, or a condition that can erode your interest in the primary purpose of being at college: to learn and to prepare for your future. The predominant philosophy on college campuses is that learning is a chore; but this is just one perspective, and not the only one. Learning, too, can be fun. Emotional preparedness means having or developing the necessary maturity to discern how to keep the right balance; mental preparedness means having the discipline to make the right choices to maintain that balance and to follow through on the mechanics. With these three levels of preparation as a start, learning can become quite enjoyable.

In fact, learning can become an exhilarating experience. People who have practiced the art of inner learning report as much. To give up too soon by avoiding discipline and balance for short-term pleasures, is to take the easy way out and to rob yourself of what can become the foundation for a lifetime of fruitful and satisfying benefits.

_____ Summary

To maximize learning, you must not only be conscientious about basic mechanical preparation, but also begin to develop the mental and emotional traits that can help you to maintain good mechanical preparation. Being familiar with the rules of a game, for example, will only help you if you develop the strategies and mental attitudes to challenge a clever opponent. Similarly, the strategies of discipline and emotional balance will help you to make the most of your paper, pen, and textbook.

In the next chapter, I will introduce you to common hindrances in college life that can block you from learning. Recognizing how to overcome them will assist you in your efforts to be prepared.

Exercise _____

Go over your own schedule, including the time you have allotted to non-academic activities, and assess how the three levels of preparation fit in. Decide what activities can be enhanced with preparation, and outline specific ways you can become prepared on the three levels for each activity.

4

External Hindrances
To Learning

In the story, *The Little Prince,* a pilot is stranded in the desert and meets a little man who claims to be the prince of another planet, who has journeyed to earth. The pilot hears many odd stories from the prince including startling observations about the people of his own world. Time runs out, however, as he tries to fix his plane before he begins to starve and dehydrate. The prince urges the pilot to accompany him across the desert in search of a well. The pilot is cautious; better to remain where he is than to set out without any guarantee of water. But the prince insists, and the pilot finally gives in, begrudgingly. They trudge into the desert, and just when it seems they have made a fatal mistake, the prince discovers the well.

This story illustrates the potential rewards of setting out on new and untested paths, such as discovering the art of inner learning, in order to find something that may improve yourself or your situation. You can be hindered in this goal by a wide variety of factors, some of which come from within, and some of which are external. You have to recognize both in order to get past them and proceed.

This chapter is a look at the external blocks to learning that students seem to complain most about, and that many psychologists acknowledge. You have already begun to learn about seeing things from new perspectives, and in this chapter you will discover additional ways in which your own talent can assist you in the classroom.

_____ The Obstructions

Rigid mindsets taught to us by others

The pilot in *The Little Prince* reminds me of a young man in an introductory philosophy course. I had used a variety of stories and devices to get the students to realize that reality could be viewed (and *is* or has been viewed in other parts of the world) from a number of diverse perspectives, from solipsism ("I am the only one who exists and everyone else is projected from my imagination") to idealism (only the mind and its perceptions exist).

I asked the young man to come up with clear proof that he was not just dreaming or simply a brain preserved in a vat of liquid, being stimulated with electrodes to have the experiences he thought he was having. He became quite hostile, grabbed the table, his breath coming fast, and shouted, "I know what reality is! Whatever I can touch and see and taste and hear and smell! That's all there is to it!"

It was not that he was necessarily right or wrong that made him stand out; it was that he was so *desperate* to maintain his ideas. This student had been trained in the educational system to believe that empirical science was "the truth," and there was nothing more to say about it. But there was more to his vehement exclamations than that. He felt the rug of his belief system slipping out from underneath him and he was afraid. He wanted things solid, unequivocal, unambiguous—guaranteed! He would not have been willing to go out with the prince in search of a well, and being unwilling, would have missed out.

An open and flexible curiosity is necessary for the mental exercise involved in learning. If something within the educational system provides that sense of permanence and security, it becomes more difficult for students to try out more daring ideas that provide less of a sense of stability. Plato's, *The Republic,* offers a vivid portrayal of this in his "Allegory of the Cave."

Here people are chained inside a cave by the neck and legs so that their heads cannot turn and their eyes must look forward toward the cave wall. Behind them is a fire and a stage. Whatever takes place on the stage casts its shadow on the wall. The acoustics of the cave are such that the sounds appear to be coming from the screen. The people who are chained all agree that the shadows they see comprise reality. They are satisfied to explore no further. They have no idea that there is a world outside the cave where the sun shines and the birds sing. Their state is the lot of people who simply believe what they see or are told, and never explore beyond that. Like the pilot in *The Little Prince* these people do not trust the uncertainty of something they cannot see, even if it offers the possibility a better world.

Now suppose someone from the outside world comes and takes a couple of the cave-dwellers by the hand. As they near the entrance of the cave, the light begins to hurt their eyes. Their resistance increases. They are moving away from darkness to the colorful, exciting outer world, but for them there is nothing but excruciating pain. They see only blinding flashes. This new world seems threatening and disturbing, and they want to return to the darkness.

Plato's parable not only teaches his theory of knowledge, but also illustrates an educational process. By definition, students are ignorant of some given subject area. Some are chained to their ignorance by the mindsets of people who want to keep them there. Ideally, the teacher has the ability and experience to draw students from ignorance to knowledge, perhaps even to wisdom. But there may be resistance. The student has been fed for a long time on beliefs pressed on him or her from parents, peers, and siblings who may be doing nothing more than casting chains around the person's neck and feet. It is the easiest path to simply believe what someone else tells you, rather than accepting the responsibility for believing something that you have really examined and found worthy. The latter requires much more effort, and *you* are answerable.

Think of a situation in your own life to which you can apply Plato's metaphor. Consider, for example, the mindset pointed out in the previous chapter, that learning is a chore. Now think about how such a mindset can affect your attitudes and performance in the classroom.

This allegory does not illustrate the fact that I or any other teacher knows "the truth." But in general, professors do have a position with regard to experience, training, and in-depth study that students do not yet possess. I do not propose that students swallow everything they hear from a person just because that person happens to teach at a college or university. Professors can be trapped into rigid mindsets as well. Plato's allegory illustrates the *ideal.* What I am encouraging here is that you think over the concept of tolerance and courage, and open yourself to new possibilities, especially in the basics of learning.

Expectations of others

We have little control over the expectations of other people. For example, your parents may be proud that you are in college. They want you to do your best. They want to be able to tell their friends about you, and this puts pressure on you to live up to their expectations, especially if they have a specific direction in mind for you. Or, you may have a favorite high school teacher who sees potential in you to do well. You do not want to disappoint people you love or respect.

Students who choose fields of interest that appear (to others) to have no clear future—such as theater or philosophy—often have to battle the pressure of expectations more so than students who choose business, law, or medicine. College is the time to grow up. While you must acknowledge the expectations that others have of you, you must also build your own. You are granted a real opportunity to "find yourself" by trying out a wide variety of subject areas and deciding what really satisfies you. The path of least resistance is to give in to pressure, and many people take it. You can still learn, but your range will be needlessly restricted and may make you restless and unhappy. You might not discover what you're really good at, or what suits you best.

Others' expectations often produce guilt and insecurity. You have been programmed to live up to your potential, to honor your parents, to be unselfish. When you begin to cut your own way, guilt is almost inevitable. It should not, however, become a lead weight, dragging you down and crippling you.

In an exercise in self-awareness, students were asked to imagine a room they would call their own, and to fill it with things that would make them comfortable. One girl had made her room into a dome with a skylight. As she described it, she suddenly realized that she had no place to hang the paintings she had done as an art student. She recognized that her fantasy room revealed deep guilt feelings over her father's disapproval of art as a vocation.

Along with guilt comes insecurity. You are trying something new and you may have to do it without the support system you are used to. That can be frightening. We all desire a sense of security and respect or reinforcement from others, but we cannot always get it. You will need to decide whether your own satisfaction in doing what you want can outweigh the potential loss of support.

Keep in mind, however, that the expectations of others often reflect their own needs: A mother wants her son to go into computer programming because she foresees his financial security. It frees her of worry for his future, as well as worry for herself—that she might have to support him when she needs him to support her. Instead he chooses English because he wants to be a writer—a most insecure field. He is fighting for self-expression and fails to see why his mother wants something that, in her view, is better for him.

Be understanding with those who want something for you that does not fit in with your own plans. You may think they want to control you, when, in fact, their desire for you has deeper psychological roots. Be sensitive while standing up for yourself. See through their eyes, and in all likelihood, you will feel less guilty for your own choices because compassion results in less tension than does anger and resistance. Do your work well. When you begin to show your competence in the career you have chosen, chances are you will win the respect of those who care about you.

Competition

There is always competition at places of higher learning. Students compete for spaces in popular courses; they compete at parties and in sporting events; they compete for recognition, but it is competition for grades that seems to be the most common complaint of many students. Although competition can goad us on to do our best, it can be destructive when it results in crippling anxiety or a sense of failure. Some students are simply too intimidated and either give in to mediocre work or simply drop out.

There is not much that can be done about the current grading process. It is too entrenched in the American educational system. But as with anything that seemingly cannot be changed, you are always free to regulate your *attitude* toward the system. This is the key to getting beyond many of the external hindrances: developing the mental flexibility to go within *yourself* for the answers. You may choose not to get involved with other students who need to know how they stand in comparison to you. Or you may compare your grades but not allow this to dominate your desire to learn the subject. I will say more about this ability in the following section, and explain how to develop it more fully for yourself.

Often students say they want to free themselves of competition when in reality what they want is freedom from anxiety. But a certain amount of anxiety is part of life. It helps us to continue striving (again, sometimes destructively) and it keeps us aware of the inevitable uncertainties of reality. Unfortunately, without the anxieties produced by competition, few students would do their best work. But you do not have to become entrapped in the system. *Self-*motivation is the key. You are in college for yourself and if you keep that in mind, you can diminish some of the negative effects of grade comparisons and peer pressure.

Poor teaching/poor text

It is likely that you will encounter someone who does not teach well, especially in universities that place predominant emphasis on research and scholarship (and most do). Teaching skills may sometimes be sacrificed. Many students simply become exasperated or retaliate by staging "bad teacher" contests to humiliate the instructor. Or they stop attending class altogether and blame their mediocre grade on the professor. This is the easy way out.

A student named Jackie once had a professor who not only could not decipher a difficult text, but had decided that he did not really want to teach. Instead, he directed students to spend class time doing exercises from the text, and was unable to tell them how or where they were going wrong. Most of the students gave up and took an "incomplete" for the course, hoping to make it up the next semester with someone else. Jackie, however, decided to learn the subject in spite of the professor. And she did, although she had to exert a great deal of extra effort to do so. Nevertheless, it was possible.

Some teachers will be incompetent. Some will be boring. Some will mumble or speak with thick accents. You need to keep in mind that a single person is not the only avenue to learning a subject. There are things you can do to overcome this problem. You can ask questions of someone else, study the text yourself, or get other resources. A poor teacher is never an excuse to keep yourself from learning.

The same can be said of a textbook. Sometimes a professor is trying something new and had little time to review it before selecting it; sometimes, the professor wrote it and does not perceive the lack of communication. If you have difficulty with the text and the professor cannot help you to surmount it, check the library for resources on a similar topic. Ask your professor to recommend the best approach to studying from the assigned text. Above all, do not simply resign yourself to getting nothing from the class because of a poorly written text. There *are* alternatives.

Good teaching/discipleship

This item may come as a surprise, but becoming overly attracted to a good professor *can* hinder you. Recall the student who had attached himself to one thinker that he respected. He wanted to know only what *that* person had to say on any subject, and thus had cut himself off from others who might have contributed to his intellectual development.

In a similar vein, some students had become disciples of a popular professor. They used the same voice inflections, the same posture, and the same facial gestures as the professor whenever they were involved in a discussion. They told the same jokes, spouted the same life principles, and developed a language that made them "insiders." It was not the fault of the professor. He was charismatic and provoked deep and careful thinking. He did not cultivate such disciples (although some do). Nevertheless, he inspired them to the point of extreme imitation, and it became clear to other members of the department that these students were learning from no one else. They attended classes, but failed to really listen to what anyone else had to say. They cut themselves off from opportunities to broaden their thinking. It exasperated the other professors. It also hindered those students from thinking for themselves.

While I say positive things about the mentor relationship in a later chapter, I do not support this sort of imitative discipleship. It is the "cookie-cutter" approach to education, molding some of the dough into duplicate forms and viewing the rest as extraneous scraps.

Poor advising/discrepancies in catalog description

Advisors are often busy with many things at once. You may get only general advising at best. You can insure for yourself a higher quality of attention by studying the catalog before you go for advice, then having very specific questions ready. Do not expect someone else to set up your life goals for you. Only you can do that. An advisor works best within a defined direction, and that direction must be set by you. You may change your mind later, but at least have some idea what you want *before* you go to advising. Otherwise, it can be like fishing in the ocean without the proper equipment. Taking charge of your own life is an important part of moving toward the benefits offered with inner learning.

In the school course catalog, there can sometimes be a discrepancy between the way a course is described and the way it is being taught. This happens for a variety of reasons. If you have a very strong desire to take a course just as it is listed, find out from the department who is teaching the course and ask whether that person made up the description being used, or make an appointment with the professor to discuss just what he or she is going to cover in the course. If you have no time for this sort of preparation, then attend the class on the first day and find out what you want to know in time to drop the course if it does not satisfy you. If you do not drop, and the course turns out to be something you did not really want, you have only yourself to blame. Take advantage of the "drop/add" period.

In other words, set goals, even if you think you will change them later, and ask questions! You must establish a direction before you can begin to exercise and develop your learning potential. External factors can confuse you. Keep your head clear by knowing what you want.

Extracurricular distractions

Every student knows what I mean by this. Sports, parties, social functions, committees, groups. There is a great deal more to the college experience than simply going to class. Each of these activities can and should be used to increase your learning experience, but should not become such a priority that they are detrimental to what you came to college for. Again, this obstacle can be best minimized or removed through your own self-management.

Lack of balance/too much to do

Sometimes students simply take on too much. One student who was very bright set out in his freshman year to create his own major. He was quite ambitious and he immersed himself with a number of difficult courses. Soon, all he was doing was studying and writing papers. His ambitions began to sour, especially when he developed other interests for which he had little or no time. Eventually he eased his load by his junior year, but had become tired and cynical. He spent an entire summer renting and watching movies (and felt guilty for it).

Another student became so involved in her sorority that her committees left her no time for her school work. She wanted the professors to give her special consideration. Some of her teachers refused. It had been her choice, they reminded her, to get overinvolved. She could have said no. She had other responsibilities, and when she shunned these, she realized the consequences. She did badly in several courses, but she learned something about balancing her activities and setting her *own* priorities.

Similarly, students involved in sports often think that being on the road to participate in intercollegiate sports gives them special status. They may ask for a passing grade even though they have done little or no work to deserve one. Such students need to remember that they are not in college primarily to play sports, and that to give them an undeserved grade is unfair to students who work hard and possibly sacrifice sports in order to do well.

Poor classroom/laboratory facilities

There is little you can do to change this. At some universities more students are assigned to a room than there is seating capacity. Desks are jammed together, the air is stifling, and there may be no windows for ventilation or for illusion of space. This is another situation in which the only thing you can control is your attitude. If you want to learn, you may have to put up with poor facilities, and do the best with what you have. Sometimes this is the road to creativity—improvising when options are limited.

_____ Summary

While you may have some control over potential external hindrances, often the only thing you can change is how you view them. If you really want to learn, you can find ways around almost any circumstantial obstacle. Keep in mind that your college or university was not set up with your personal needs and desires in mind. You will have to set your own goals and find ways to achieve them. The resources are available, but it will often be up to you to match them to your own ambitions. You may feel devalued as a person, helpless, and out of control, but the educational system is not responsible *for* you, only *to* you. There is a big difference. Once you realize this difference, you will understand your own responsibilities for your education.

Exercise _____

1. Consider how the hindrances listed in the text apply to you.
2. If you think there are external hindrances that have not been covered, make up your own list, either from what you anticipate or from what you have experienced in other situations (e.g., from high school). Imagine ways to overcome them.

5

Internal Hindrances
To Learning

R eorganizing your attitudes can assist you with many
external blocks to learning, but internal blocks are
often not as obvious, nor as easy to overcome. Nevertheless, they can interfere just as much or more than the
external blocks. Again, this list is not definitive but it may
give you an idea of the most common problem areas for
people in your circumstances.

_____ The Internal Obstacles

Fear of failure/fear of success

Probably the most common psychological interference to
entertaining new ideas is the fear that we will not succeed
at something for which we have no track record, and thus
no clear verification of our abilities. It is easier to believe
in yourself when you have already accomplished something
similar to what you are now approaching. If you have never
had a philosophy or a physics course, you might avoid
taking one and concentrate instead on computers, with
which you feel more comfortable. You may, however, be
depriving yourself of discovering talents and interests you
did not imagine you had.

Your college years present opportunities that you may
never again have to try something new. You may fail at
them. On the other hand, you may reap more success—
even with the threat of failure—than if you stayed with the
familiar subjects. Continuous success results in complacency.

In Kierkegaard's terminology, you need to take a "leap of
faith," be willing to "float over ten thousand leagues of
water," to take a risk. Although people who have a record

of success may have some advantage because they may possess more confidence, everyone who tries a new subject needs courage and perseverance. And above all, if you do stumble a bit, you must remember that we *all* stumbled in order to learn how to walk.

People tend to view failure as a dead end, or even as an indication that they *themselves* are losers. Yet what some people count as failure can be interpreted as simply the life process of sorting things out, of learning what doesn't work in order to get on with what does. All successful people experience setbacks. Even Einstein went up some blind alleys. The difference between successful people and those who just give up, is that they are able to turn an apparent failure into a step toward success. It requires mental agility, and techniques for developing this skill are offered in the next section as part of the art of inner learning.

The flip side of this fear is the fear of success. Jerry was a student who seemed to have more potential for success than what he displayed in the classroom. He seemed unhappy about holding back, yet also unable to allow himself to put forth his best effort. When questioned, it became clear that he measured himself by his father's success. His father had never been to college, and Jerry could not bring himself to surpass him!

Success brings new experiences, unexplored opportunities, even new dimensions to your personality. While we all strive for it, many are unprepared for the unfamiliar new world into which they are entering. It is important to try to envision, in concrete terms, just what "success" will mean to you, so that when you achieve it, you will have made yourself comfortable with it. Visualization exercises, offered in the next section, will assist you with developing this ability.

Self-criticism

Some people have a tendency to be negative. We hear more often about mistakes we make than about things we have done well. This can lead to seeing ourselves as less than we are, which, in turn, can set us up for achieving less than we want. Some people in this position develop forms of "self-talk" that keep them from going beyond what they believe they can do. They say things like:

"You're so stupid."

"What makes you think you can tackle a subject as difficult as calculus?"

"You've never been any good at anything. Why don't you just drop out now and save the expense?"

These are just some examples. While I am not advocating a "positive thinking" approach that blinds you to genuine limitations, I do think the successful student must practice self-affirmation and self-encouragement as part of self-mastery. Many courses in college are *not* easy, and will challenge even the brightest person. You need to realize just how you might hinder yourself with negative "self-talk" so that you can later take advantage of ways to channel mental energy from negative to positive comments. Self-criticism betrays a lack of trust in yourself. Trust is something over which you have control. You *can* change your attitude, as you should have discovered in doing the exercises in Chapter 2. Focusing on positive traits that you have can encourage you to live up to what you believe about yourself. You will get more exposure to this in the next chapter.

Need for control

While I advocate finding ways to control how you choose to participate in your education, it cannot be denied that a psychological *need* for control can actually be a hindrance.

A student named Steve had a job as a resident assistant in a college dormitory. Part of that job included night security. The front door was open twenty-four hours, but after two o'clock, only dorm residents were allowed in. Steve had to check ID cards for each person entering, and keep a log of their names.

When he started the job, he insisted on doing it by the

letter, checking cards even of people he knew. Sometimes they did not have their cards and, playing by the book, Steve was faced with having to lock them out. It seemed ridiculous. He waved them through because he knew they belonged there. Eventually the rigid manner in which he approached the job struck him as being rather silly. If he waved certain people through on one night, why not anytime? The idea behind the rule was to screen for non-residents, yet Steve had become so obsessed with doing the job to the letter that he had failed to see that such rigidity was not only unnecessary, but hindered him from establishing rapport with the residents.

The need for control is present in everyone, to one degree or another. We want a sense of security, of permanence, and the *feeling* that we are in control seems to give it to us. That can be a positive source of motivation, as well as a crippling obsession. Some people slip easily into belief systems that offer the illusion of permanence, while others actively manipulate their world to assure themselves that, should anything change, they can control just how it will change. This need, however, can interfere with learning. Allowed to become extreme, it can narrow our perspective and strip us of a willingness to take any positive risks.

For example, when choosing your major, you may gravitate toward subjects that give you a sense of stability without really understanding that your choice has more to do with a hidden need than with something you really want. You may opt for something that you *know* will ensure a job after college, or a high salary, rather than allowing yourself to look into subject areas that may interest you and in which you may have great ability, but which frightens you with its potential uncertainty. Understanding your *needs* can help you to better distinguish between true choices and neurotic drives disguised as choice.

The irony of the need to control is that it can backlash to the point that you actually *lose* control *to* your need. The tragedy is that clinging to control develops impatience, irritation, and rigidity, all of which block the mind from exploration, discovery, and flexibility.

Being in control as a result of a desperate need for security does not necessarily get you the best results (despite the fact that it may be one of the reasons you seek control). The need to be in control is often the result of feeling threatened. You are not sure what you are up against, so you become cautious and close off as many "unknown" factors as possible. You also close off potential learning opportunities.

Wanting to be in control can push you into trying too hard. There is an art to achieving fruitful concentration in which you are exercising self-discipline and self-control. Attempting to *force* it pushes you *past* it to needless frustration (and minimal learning). Good concentration requires relaxation, but the need for control undermines this condition. Learn the difference between desiring control as a form of security and desiring it as a way to take responsibility for yourself. One can harm you, the other will help.

Boredom

It is almost inevitable that you will take some subjects that will bore you. Remaining bored is a childish attitude of passive expectation that others will make things interesting for you. It is a failure to live up to your potential and to discover and tap your own resources.

Marilyn stumbled into college by accident. She was visiting friends, saw a summer schedule at the University, thought some of the courses looked interesting, and signed up. She enjoyed it so much, she decided to stay for a year and take more courses. Eventually she received a degree in psychology and philosophy, and had taken a dozen courses more than she even needed. Why? Because she was *interested*. She took every course that seemed the least bit stimulating, from Theater to Nutrition. She studied languages, minored in Comparative Literature and took far more courses in her major than was necessary. She even went to noncredited meetings at night for those who wanted concentrated study on some particular subject. It seemed to everyone who knew her that she had more time and energy than they did, but the real difference was that she made the most of her time and actually *gained* energy by tapping internal resources through being motivated to keep learning. For Marilyn, college was one of the best experiences she ever had. Why? Because she was *interested*!

In contrast to Marilyn, Karen allowed herself to become bored. Like Marilyn, she had a few professors who were not very effective in the classroom. Marilyn's approach was to go beyond the classroom and find out about the subjects for herself. Karen, however, became bored with the uninspired presentations. She decided to skip class rather than endure. She missed out on learning about several subjects that might have interested her had she given them more effort. The resources were there. She simply failed to take advantage of them. It was easier to give in to boredom and blame the teacher. But it was as much her fault.

Boredom prevents you from enjoying what you are doing. One of the key elements to developing the art of inner learning is enjoyment, and if you insist on being bored, you will hinder yourself from getting involved.

College students often do not realize that time passes quickly and there is simply no time to be bored! Nor any reason for it. Boredom is one thing you can control. If you are required to take an apparently boring subject, find something in it that will be valuable to other subjects you are studying. Or find a way to learn about it outside a boring textbook. If you have a poor professor, get what you can from that person but do not limit yourself to his or her lectures. Such limitations are self-imposed. If you are bored, it is a result of your own attitude.

The bored mind retains little or nothing. It is like people holding their breath in the middle of a fragrant garden. Such minds make no differentiations, and can take in only superficial perceptions, at best. They are lazy minded. You will quickly find that you have no long-term recall from courses in which you allowed boredom to dominate.

As a young child you were probably rarely, if ever, bored. You can approach your college studies with the mind of a child because the joy of learning can be much like the joy of play, as you will learn in the next section of this book.

Popularity

I once had an older student in a class say something like, "We live to die. There's nothing more." His comment proved to be unpopular with the majority of students and they tried to shut him out of the rest of the discussion. The professor invited him to say more about his position, so the man explained his reasons for why he had said what he had. The reasons were more tolerable to the other students than the initial statement and they began to ask him more questions, even though they had originally dismissed him.

It is difficult to stand alone. Too often the need to be popular, to say what everyone would agree with, works like a muzzle. Students simply say nothing, or repeat what has already been said. Both responses are unproductive.

If you fail to express your thoughts and opinions, you never get the chance to try them out. Only if they are challenged or questioned will you have the opportunity to build a defense (and thus understand your own ideas better) or to discard an idea as unfruitful.

If you are the kind of person who wants to talk but only says what has already been said, you waste everyone's time and soon become exasperating. Imitation for the sake of being accepted only digs you deeper into ignorance, and may make you prone to supporting faulty beliefs.

In the learning process, the motivation to be popular is largely erosive. You don't take risks. It is important to be liked and to make friends, but a balance must be achieved.

Worry

Worry is part of human nature. Some things are worth worrying about because they produce positive action, like getting treatment for a health condition. Other worries are more mundane, like worrying about whether you received a better grade on a paper than did your roommate. They only drain you of energy that might more profitably be spent concentrating on your studies. It would be fruitless to attempt to list here all of the worries that plague college students. The list would never end. What you must do, if you want to prevent worry from eroding your productivity is to divide your concerns into those that you can do something about (e.g., like choosing a major that satisfies you), and those over which you have no control, or that only create unproductive stress.

Mental constipation

You might encounter what writer's call "writer's block," where you simply cannot seem to study, or if you study, you cannot retain anything. Typically, just taking a break helps. This may mean an hour for pizza or a semester off to read, work, or travel. However, if you insist that you simply cannot take such breaks, sometimes it helps just to go through the motions of studying. Open your book, scan the pages, take notes. Your ability to retain and to think over what you are reading may return through good habits. Otherwise you may need to seek counseling for blocks that may not be apparent.

Poor self-image

How we view ourselves affects what we think and what we do. The young man who saw himself in his father's shadow kept himself from potential success that might have been satisfying to him. He did not know his own stengths and weaknesses because he saw only his father's. He had no real self-image, certainly none that could motivate him toward success in college.

Some students feel they can only be "average." They have been told this by teachers and parents, and have gotten it into their heads that a label makes them who they are. They identify with the expectations of others, and thus "can't" do anything but what others have declared they can do. This sort of self-crippling has been demonstrated over and over again in research. Yet low expectations for yourself are the result of your *own* self definition. It is *you* who decides to adopt for yourself someone else's label. Others might be wrong about you, unless you *allow* them to be right. Of course, making up your own mind is easier said than done, especially for people who are insecure about how they judge themselves, but it *can* be done. It *is* possible. Even if the opinions of others seem overwhelming, it is still *you* who accepts them. At the very least, you can *try out* a new, more positive label and see how it feels.

Of course, there is always the chance that you can be wrong about yourself, too. Accuracy of self-perception can be distorted. We can be blind to things about ourselves that are true. The key is to become more self-aware and sensitive to the *possibility* that others *may* be right about us, but to stand up for ourselves if their judgements are calculated to take us down a notch rather than to assist us in improving ourselves. In Chapter 7, I will offer you a technique for becoming more self-aware and less prone to misleading labels imposed upon you by others.

There is no easy way to know who is right, but keep your focus on motivating yourself to do the work necessary to improve your chances for developing the art of inner learning. This may require that you develop confidence in your own value, or it may mean that you slacken up on overconfidence. Either way, you must be prepared to see how your self-image is a factor in how you approach your learning experience.

Selective perception

Other people may see something we miss because we are thinking so strongly along other tracks that we neglect the opportunity to see from a new perspective. Timothy Gallway, in his book, *The Inner Game of Tennis* describes a time when his wife mentioned how like the moon was a tennis ball in motion. He was confused so she described the way the shadows on the ball begin to eclipse the ball. He still failed to understand until they began to play again and he focused on what his wife had pointed out rather than on running, swinging his racket or judging net shots. To his surprise, he saw the shadows. He had concentrated on the ball many times, but had failed to see this rather obvious feature. His mind had been preoccupied with other aspects of watching the ball.

The same thing can happen in the classroom. You don't hear or notice something that is right there in front of you because you become preoccupied with other things. You may be distracted by outside activities or by something about the very subject that you are studying. Whatever the case, a selective mind can miss something important, or even just something interesting.

We are all prone to some amount of selective perception. We cannot concentrate on everything at once, so we take in only the things that are meaningful to us. However, it is all too easy to limit our vision and thus limit our learning experience. Develop the habit of broadening your perspective and looking for more than you might ordinarily see. You may find things you had never imagined. I provide exercises for this as part of the art of inner learning in the next section, in the chapter on "Mental Agility."

Cluttered mind

While it may seem contradictory to follow advice to broaden your perspective with advice on becoming more focused, there is a way you can achieve both. To focus your mind, you need goals that can help you set priorities and can keep you from trying to do so much at once that you lose sight of what you want to achieve. However, at the same time you set goals, you can assess whether you are ignoring some worthwhile perspective on what you are thinking or learning. To give another perspective some attention is not necessarily to lose focus, but simply to see if there is something there that can assist you. For example, you may wish to become a biologist, so you set up a schedule with science courses that will help you achieve your goal. However, you may also discover something worthwhile in a less obvious course, such as history or creative writing. Your goal helps you turn your schedule into a focused breadth rather than more clutter.

It is also the case that some people are more prone to being too selective, while others are prone to taking on too much, thus cluttering their minds. In that case, you can see the items above as two different forms of advice for two different problem areas.

Inability to listen

Inability to listen can result from many things, one of which is simply poor concentration habits. Improving your concentration goes hand-in-hand with improving your listening skills and your capacity for inner learning. You will hear more about this in the next section.

However, sometimes poor listening is the result of "knowing too much." This is the cluttered mind, mentioned earlier. You already "know" so you don't need to pay attention. The only cure for this attitude is for you to realize that, much as you may be familiar with any given subject, you do not know everything. As with the tennis player who was intimately familiar with the ball in play from years of experience, you may be missing the shadows.

Poor listening also comes from lack of preparation. I once taught a course called "Philosophies of Death and Dying;" one evening, the topic was suicide. I attempted to get a discussion going but heard mostly vague and ill-formed comments from a handful of those attending. When I attempted to draw them to the articles assigned, I realized that they were not listening. I asked how many had read the assignment. Three of forty-six students raised their hands! There was no point in continuing. They had no context for grasping the lecture, nor for substantial discussion. They were not listening well because they did not understand the lecture material. The "cure" for this should be obvious.

Fear of exposure

Many students feel insecure, even into their senior year. They may acknowledge the value of involvement in discussion, yet never say a word because they are afraid of exposing their ideas to others. This is the inner side of the pressure to become popular mentioned in the last chapter. Typically this fear is rooted in a need for affirmation—to hear from others that their thoughts and ideas *are* reasonable, acceptable, perhaps even interesting.

Sarah was a student in a "Medical Ethics" course. She sat in the back of the room, dutifully taking notes, but silent as a mouse. After one class, she approached the professor and asked a question about some point in the discussion. Her question was perceptive and astute, and would have added dimension to the discussion had she asked it in class. But she was too shy, she admitted, to speak out. Several times during the semester, she came up with interesting questions or comments. Yet never once did she allow her mind to connect with other students. She deprived them of her intelligent thoughts. She was simply too frightened that her ideas would not be well received. Despite assurance from the professor that she had worthwhile ideas, Sarah was never quite confident that the "next one" would be as good.

Like control, the fear of exposure can be motivated by a desperate need: confirmation of your opinions. The fear can intimidate you so much that you deprive yourself of opportunities to get that need met. It is a debilitating distrust of your abilities.

Try out your ideas. I have never seen a student thrown out the door for an expressed opinion. Try to imagine the worst possible scenario for an event where you say what you are thinking. Then imagine yourself living with the consequences of that event. Reinterpret the imagined response as evidence of problems that *other* students have accepting opinions that are different from their own. The sooner you get over your fear of exposure to potential ridicule, the sooner you will be in a position to receive the respect that you seek. And, by finding out which of your ideas are illogical or poorly supported you will be able to put them aside and focus on the good ideas you have; and you can only find these out by expressing them. Focusing on your good ideas will win you affirmation, and plant the seeds for self-confidence.

Beware, however, of allowing your desire for affirmation to become so great that you become obsessed by it. As with control, find the balance that assists you rather than hinders you in the classroom.

Frustration/intolerance

Peter entered college with the attitude that he might not get much of value out of his courses. When he went to class, he sat rigidly, his jaw tense and his mind prepared to shut out anything but what he thought he wanted to hear. He argued with the professors before he even understood what they had said. He had done a lot of reading and he knew what he wanted to hear. Anything else was a waste of time.

Peter was frustrated. Day after day, he received less and less stimulation from attending class. So he attended class less and less. His mind squeezed shut on the things he already knew, and that became his world. As you can imagine, Peter's grades suffered. He learned to rationalize his failure as the failure of the system, of his professors, of the way the classes were organized. He decided that college was not a place to learn, so he buried himself in books he had already read, and allowed nothing more to penetrate his beliefs.

He is a clear illustration that the source of our frustration is often *us*. We like to blame it on other things, but until we look around and within ourselves to find what we might be able to change to relieve the frustration, we cannot fairly or honestly attribute it to external sources.

Frustration is the result of an attitude—*how* you look at something. And as you already know, the way you approach any situation reveals something about *you*. Stress management research indicates that strong emotions like frustrations can be controlled and even diminished by changing your mind about how you will approach a potentially frustrating situation. Not everyone reacts to the same situation in the same way, which means it is not the *situation* that is frustrating, but the *person* who is frustrated. Standing in long lines for financial aid, for example, can be viewed as an opportunity to meet new people or get some reading done.

Likewise, in the classroom learning is your responsibility. Remain flexible and get what you can out of each learning situation. Frustration blocks you from achieving that, but it is you who decides whether or not to be frustrated. The alert, eager mind is the mind most capable of getting past these blocks and focusing on the real goals.

Need for concrete answers, structure, practicality

Some courses will resonate closely with your personality; others will not. In philosophy courses, many students are there for *the* answer to difficult and slippery questions. What is truth? What is reality? How should I live my life? Is there a God? What happens after I die? They want an answer. The multiple possibilities of ambiguity and open-endedness are too frightening. So after their first philosophy course, where "the answer" is not forthcoming, students return to math courses, engineering, computer programming, or sciences where they feel more comfortable.

Yet to be truly educated means that you become willing to expose yourself to subjects which do not fit neatly into your vision of things. Why? Because your vision of things may be too limited. As with intolerance, the fear of abstract reasoning can shut you out of opportunities to broaden your understanding.

The same goes for philosophy students who love abstract mental chess games so much that they shy away from the concrete and practical. A professor once asked a group of senior philosophy majors to focus on the concrete details of their experience. They were extremely resistant, wanting to launch back into their heady theoretical discussions, where they felt safe—another form of a structured world. They limited their understanding of the world as much as did the students who demanded concrete structure and practicality.

Perfectionism/overconfidence

Perfectionism is not limited to students who achieve the best grades. It is a manifestation of our vision of ourselves, which can be accurate or inaccurate, depending on how great a hindrance our need is for perfection,

Janet was a leader. She did everything to the best of her ability, but she was continually dissatisfied because nothing she did was ever exactly right. She strove to achieve this goal. The better she did, the more confidence she gained that eventually she would really shine forth in all of her activities. She took several courses with me and did very well. However, during her third time with me, I changed my approach, and required something of her for which she had no "record of success." It frightened her. The possibility for doing only a competent job loomed all too clearly. Rather than make herself vulnerable to a "fall from grace," she dropped the course.

Janet is like many other students. I have heard some students say that if they did not get an "A" in some course, they would drop it. That is, they assured themselves of a 4.0 record by taking only courses in which they could get an "A." What such students fail to realize is that the 4.0 record may stamp them as "excellent students," but they are only selectively and superficially educated. They are not really learning how to be *students*, but how to play the system. Their real skill lies in figuring out what courses they can excel in and what courses to avoid. Those they avoid, however, are those for which they have closed off their learning opportunities and limited their vision.

Poor motivation/lack of discipline/lack of goals

A common complaint of students is that they "just can't get going." Discipline is something they can learn, but not without motivation to learn it. Discipline is a demanding taskmaster, and without *inner* motivation, external motivation becomes a burden rather than a facilitating influence.

Dr. Charles Garfield, an expert on the concept of "peak performance," claims in his book, *Peak Performers: The New Heroes of American Business,* "Our peak performers consistently told us that external motivators produce the shortest-lived results. Such motivations work by promising reward or punishment; and when the reward is no longer novel, or the punishment disappears, so does the behavior that was associated with it."

So how does one get motivated to learn? By making learning *intrinsically* rewarding and personally worthwhile, which is what the second section of this book is about. To become educated involves an individual decision to make a commitment to learning. It involves knowing your responsibilities and living up to them. It involves energy and focus. In our society, however, those words have taken on negative connotations by people who dislike sacrifice, and who seek only short-term satisfactions. Again, they are negative only within a context of someone's *values* that make them negative.

Developing good learning habits can not only help you in your career, but can help you achieve satisfying diversions in your personal life, for the rest of your life. Building motivation involves a long-term vision. Know what you want and decide what it takes to get you there; along the way, develop ways to gain fulfillment.

Motivation is also strengthened by the process of obtaining your goals. The process pays off through the acquisition of productive learning skills as well as through a personal sense of achievement.

Refusal to examine self

If you are unaware of things about yourself that can hinder your achievement of educational goals, those things will not change and will continue to hinder you. Sometimes as the result of over-confidence, insecurity, or fear, students ignore the benefits of broadening their self-awareness. Don't let discomfort block you. Self-awareness is a beneficial tool that can help you get *past* the discomfort and towards something positive. You will appreciate the value more clearly when you read Chapter 7.

In the context of self-awareness, you should also know what personality traits have been identified by psychologists as those that can assist you in achieving success with the art of inner learning. They are listed in the next chapter.

Summary

We all have psychological blocks that can weaken or hinder our ability to achieve our goals. As a college student, you have a limited amount of time. The college environment is a good place to examine yourself for problem areas that you may wish to change. The list above is not exhaustive but may help you to see things in yourself that you want to work on. Understanding and working with traits that can undermine your intentions or hold you back will give you a greater appreciation for and attunement to your strengths.

Exercise

1. Return to the list you developed in Chapter 1 and use it to help you make a preliminary assessment of the things

you may be doing to sabotage your ability to learn. Make a list for yourself, keeping in mind that such a list may not be complete (or even entirely accurate). Use this as a "working assessment" to give yourself a general direction for understanding the ideas involved in later chapters.

6

Characteristics That Facilitate Learning

Not only is it important to understand features of your experience that prevent you from getting the most out of the classroom, but you must also be able to identify those qualities that you possess or need to strive to develop that will *assist* you. Again, the list is not definitive, but it will give you a good idea. It is based on research with people who exhibit quality and excellence in what they do and who advocate the sense of seemingly effortless achievement that results from work performed at peak ability. Many of these traits are the positive side of the learning blocks listed in the previous chapter.

Psychologist Mihaly Csikzentmihalyi talks about the "autotelic self" in his book, *Flow: the Psychology of Optimal Experience,* as a quality in people who can summon at will the ability to shape the quality of their own lives, regardless of what is happening externally. This is the sort of person who is most likely to be able to practice the art of inner learning. Such people possess many of the following characteristics.

Openmindedness

In college, you will be exposed to ideas and beliefs that are not only foreign to you but might actually be repugnant or frightening. If you have already made up your mind, for example, that abortion is murder, you might be incensed at people in an ethics course offering agruments for the other side, and vice versa. In order to learn, you need to be open to at least understanding a broader spectrum of ideas and perspectives than you are used to hearing. If everyone agreed on everything, there would be little motivation to develop and refine ideas.

It is important to remember that to listen to another idea does not mean that you have to accept it, or that it will invade your own belief system. If you are truly afraid to hear something that "goes against the grain" for you, then perhaps you are not so sure of the validity of your own beliefs.

Listening to other ideas and being open to understanding them can draw you into new worlds of experience, which are not necessarily frightening. Suppose you had come to the conclusion that you were not talented in math because you had tried it once before and failed. Then suppose someone said to you that the method you used was not the only method available. If you were open to learning a different method, you might discover talents you never knew you had. You might even discover your future career!

Jennifer came into a science fiction class already comfortable with and confident of her own beliefs. She listened to the professor politely but never really heard what he was saying because she was so sure of herself. If *she* was right, she felt, then other ideas had to be wrong. At one point, the professor introduced a perspective that he felt gave the subject a new and unusual angle. Jennifer began to argue with him that such an approach was ridiculous; it did not fit well with her own beliefs. He encouraged her to give it a chance, but she refused. She spent the rest of the semester arguing with him.

The next semester, she took a sociology course. The same perspective was offered, and she realized that, had she listened in the first place, she'd have some advantage in the course. Finally she loosened up enough to learn, then realized to her own surprise how much she actually *liked* this new perspective—that it gave her exciting ideas about her own life! She wished she had been open enough to have learned it when she first had the opportunity.

I've often heard college graduates moan about how

much they missed when they were in college, and wish for such unique opportunities again. Cultivating openmindedness right away can have real advantages for you.

_____ Self-awareness

Self-awareness helps you to realize how your beliefs came into being, and how your responses and reactions are shaped by those beliefs. One of the obstacles to learning that I mentioned was the refusal to take stock of your individual tastes and biases. Your perspective is based on your values, which then feeds into your behavior (for example, a prejudice prevents you from working in a group with a person from another race). Your initial values may not have been chosen for you, but becoming aware of them allows you the choice to maintain them or not. It makes sense, then, that cultivating self-awareness would be on the list of qualities belonging to people who open themselves up to learning.

You may know the difference between people who are self-aware and people who are not. As with everything, there is a negative side, and you can exaggerate the practice of self-awareness to the point of mental paralysis, examining everything in such detail that you fail to see beyond it. Remember that self-awareness is a tool to be developed to aid you in learning, it is *not* an end in itself.

_____ Tolerance

Tolerance means flexibility: you possess the ability to listen to other people and to suspend judgment about what they say. Tolerance goes beyond being merely open to new ideas; it involves the ability to understand them and allow them to exist side-by-side with your own. Students who have received a very dogmatic upbringing or who get involved in organizations that practice a narrow, exclusive perspective may have trouble learning how to allow other people to have and express their own opinions, like Larry below.

Larry found himself assigned to a group whose task it was to coordinate a position on a controversial issue. The group chose to discuss the drinking age. Larry balked. He did not think this was much of an issue and could not believe that the other four members of his group did. Finally he had to yield to the majority and he worked on it only begrudgingly. He found himself constantly at odds with the others in the group because he did not agree with their opinion and he felt that they were stupid for not sharing his. He never listened to their reasons nor did he respond to their efforts to get him involved. He simply could not tolerate people who did not think the way he did. As a consequence he missed out on learning about what they thought as well as learning how to work as a team. He also neglected the potential for associating with the others outside of class.

Tolerance also means you have the ability to "reframe" ideas or statements in order to see them from various perspectives. Reframing means to see something in a way other than how it first appears. Psychologists Richard Bandler and John Grinder say in *Trance-Formations* that "the meaning of any event depends upon the 'frame' in which we perceive it. When we change the frame, we change the meaning . . . When the meaning changes, the person's responses and behaviors also change." For example, "group work" can be reframed as "the coordination of the strengths of several people for greater breadth and effort on the assigned task." An idea that seems repugnant to you can be reframed as an opportunity to discover something about yourself that makes this idea so offensive. Students who practice flexibility have a greater chance of learning a broad range of concepts than those who insist on focusing on only their own point of view.

Alert, Eager Mind

No matter how tolerant, self-aware and open you are, you will not get far without developing an attitude of eagerness to learn. It is not a matter of just going to class and deciding that you will listen fairly to what others have to say. That has value, of course, but does not really engage you actively or enthusiastically in your pursuit of learning.

Think of a subject that interests you. What is it like for you? It is very likely that you enjoy learning about it and are always ready to hear more, like reading a good book that motivates you to keep turning the page.

Now think of a subject that bores you. How does your attitude and behavior differ from the subject that you enjoy? Undoubtedly, you try to avoid the boring subject, put off studying to the last minute, drag yourself to class complaining, and are only happy when you're free of it. Comparing the two cases should give you a clear picture of why an eager mind facilitates learning.

Sustaining eagerness is easier if your mind is alert. When you are alert, you are more likely to notice the fine details that elude a lethargic mind.

_____ Energy

An active mind requires energy. Learning is an activity that involves effort. The need to keep your energy levels high cannot be overstated. Energy is a physical product of taking care of yourself by eating right, sleeping well, and getting exercise. In the book, *Mentally Tough,* Dr. James Loehr, who teaches the art of peak performance, insists that one of the essential ingredients is physical health and stamina, because your energy level will be determined by what you do for and with your body.

_____ Vision

Vision is another aspect of reframing. You see more or farther than others see because you are willing to explore the value of any given situation. People with vision can find opportunities where others see nothing at all.

The inventor of velcro was inspired by an annoying activity we've all experienced: pulling burrs from socks. This person had vision. Great inventions frequently arise from situations to which people normally give no thought. Exercising vision in the classroom does not require a revamping of the education system, but can happen in smaller ways.

For example, a group of students assigned to prepare an argument about an important social issue chose to explore the topic of automobile insurance reform. They could present their argument in any argument format they chose, and so they envisioned a way that would not only make the work interesting and fun for them, but would make their topic memorable and provocative to the rest of the class. One group member suggested they put on a science fiction skit about a spaceship crew from the future who were so strapped by insurance payments that they decided to travel back in time (to what was the present for the students) to find out how the system had become such a mess. At first the other group members resisted, as they were reluctant to try an approach so dramatically different from anything previously done in that class. However, they decided to give it a try. The skit captivated the audience's attention and was a huge success. The person who had suggested it had seen beyond the typical presentation format, and devised a unique means for getting the ideas across. The discussion that followed from the rest of the class was more lively than any of the other presentations. This was an exercise of vision; first by a lone voice who dared to suggest it, and then by the rest of the group, who decided to follow through.

In the next section you will learn about getting beyond appearances in order to see what others fail to see. You will also learn about developing mental flexibility. Both of these skills will assist you in cultivating vision.

Ability to Set Goals

"Although meaning for each of us is unique and subject to change," says psychologist Terry Orlick, "it seems to flow more readily when we are striving toward some goal that we find worthy." You will get nowhere if you have no idea where you want to go. Although I have been discussing the importance of the process over the end result, you still need both. Process goals—stages along the way toward achieving your success—have no direction apart from the ultimate goals; but final goals can soon become demanding taskmasters if you do not find fulfillment as well in the process of getting to them.

In the context of this book, we are discussing the goal of success in the college classroom, and the way to get there is to practice the art of inner learning. The process goals are outlined along the way, e.g., developing motivations and self-awareness, being prepared, knowing your strengths. In the next section you will learn a few more. As you realize these goals, you will move toward the achievement of your ultimate goal, although "success" must still be determined by you.

Part of motivation includes receiving feedback on how well you are progressing. Unless you have goals against which to measure yourself, you will have no idea. You will be unable to set clear priorities in your behavior, or steer yourself in clear directions. You may end up wandering through school rather aimlessly.

Setting goals requires some degree of self-awareness. You need to know what you can achieve. If you set your goals too high, you will only feel frustrated. If you set them too low, you will not reap all the possible benefits available, or discover how far you can go. You will also become bored. If you want to settle for doing average work, you may never know that you could have done something quite superior or creative.

Goals offer both purpose and motivation. To be most effective in your life, they should be chosen by you, rather than by someone else. Those most able to benefit from the art of inner learning are those who know what they want from developing these skills. You participate in your education one way or another. You can do so inefficiently by deciding on passive or undisciplined behavior, or you can get the most by developing active self-mastery that comes with inner-generated activities.

Setting goals will depend on your desires, needs, and values. If you have not yet thought about why you are in college, take time *now* to write down what you want and what you believe you need.

_____ Ability to Take Risk

Learning involves change on some level. Change can involve risk, especially change that can have impact on your life directions. We tend to avoid risk because it signals a threat to our sense of security. The thought of risk is uncomfortable and even frightening. However, making a change that results in improving a situation or a character trait gives the notion of risk a more positive angle.

Progress usually involves disrupting the status quo. Because the majority of people prefer to leave things as they are, taking a stand on an issue can mean acting against the popular voice. But the failure to take such a risk can give one a false sense of security and can ultimately lead to undesirable consequences. You may, for example, risk losing future benefits if you avoid the risks that can move you toward acquiring them.

This applies to the art of inner learning. Going beyond traditional educational practices to develop a new approach to learning is a risk. You have no idea, until you practice the new approach, what it can do for you. No matter which method you decide on, you may fear you will lose something. Either way, you take a risk.

The person who is successful in developing independent thinking, flexibility, and creativity—aspects of the art of inner learning—accepts the risks involved, because that person realizes that risks can result in positive change and potential rewards.

_____ Internal Reward System

If you are motivated at all, you will either be self-motivated or motivated by some external force. Many people do things either to get rewards or to escape pain or punishment. Students might get good grades simply to please their parents or to avoid disapproval. They may be in college for the same reasons. However, such people are trapped. They perform according to the expectations and actions of others. They are not acting freely, and have no control over their own lives. As pointed out in the last chapter, external rewards soon lose their force and motivation drops, along with performance and satisfaction.

The art of inner learning requires that you exercise freedom of choice. As with learning any complex skill, you will need perseverance, and perseverance is best developed within one's *own* system of motivation.

You can develop an internal system of rewards by setting your own goals and by developing a self-awareness that allows you to decide how much of your life is lived by you and how much by someone else. Too much dependence on others will prevent you from exercising the sort of self-encouragement you need to get past the initial effort involved in re-orienting yourself to inner learning.

Inner Discipline

Part of self-motivation involves a continuous source of encouragement that builds discipline, as pointed out in Chapter 1. Discipline helps you set and maintain priorities that are essential to achieving your goals. To maintain discipline is to put your perseverance to the test by committing yourself to action. It is your own form of training, like that of an athlete, that will make you mentally prepared for top performance and its resulting satisfaction.

The art of inner learning means that you *care* about exerting control over your life, and that you realize that mastery over your mind and body, keeping healthy and focused, has its rewards. It toughens you and makes you better able to perform. "What we do best or most perfectly," said Henry David Thoreau, "is what we have most thoroughly learned by the longest practice."

Realistic Beliefs

Part of setting goals and developing effective discipline is to acknowledge the realities around and within you.

Gary believed that he was a good communicator. However, whenever he wrote papers or answers to essay questions, his professors consistently told him that his grammar was poor and his meaning unclear. Instead of acknowledging the problems with his writing and getting help, he ignored the feedback around him and continued to believe that he was a good communicator. He did not do well in college, or in his career afterward.

There are times when it is important to think independently and to stand up for yourself, despite popular opinion. However, you must also be able to listen to others and at least give some credence to what they have to say. Something like communication requires that a speaker make sense to a listener, and grammar is not a matter of taste. You need to know the difference between being independent and being dense or stubborn. Part of developing self-awareness means observing and responding thoughtfully to the world around you, and that means acknowledging what others say about you, evaluating it, and *then* deciding how you will act. Deciding such things in a self-absorbed vacuum will not be beneficial to you in the context of learning.

Similarly, you must confront the uncomfortable realities of your learning environment. A poorly written course text book can hinder your ability to learn a subject if you decide to pretend that it is adequate simply because you are unsure about how to find other resources. Unless you take the initiative to change the situation, you may be robbing yourself of an opportunity to learn a subject that can actually excite you, given the chance.

Confronting reality may be difficult and may require extra effort to make yourself or your environment more accessible to learning, but if you want to develop an *attitude* of learning, you must face up to such things.

Ability to Reframe Setbacks

Almost every success story involves a setback. Some people label setbacks as failures. Others regard them as challenges. How you deal with setbacks in your education will influence how much you get from your college experience.

A setback should not cripple you; it should not be the last word in a situation. If you prepare yourself for the possibility of a setback, it will *not* be the last word. For example, perhaps you have been waiting to get into a popular computer course and when you finally get in, you become so confused that you cannot function with the ease that you had envisioned. You could view this experience as a failure and drop out of the course, or you could use the situation to motivate yourself into finding ways to deal with your confusion, thus uncovering inner resources you never knew you had.

Suppose you receive comments on a paper that you do not like. You could allow yourself to get depressed and feel like a failure, or you could regard the situation as a setback that signals the need for more effort or greater creativity next time. *How* you view a setback is up to you. Part of developing your capacity to practice inner learning means taking control of situations that might otherwise control you; how you label a situation can make a difference in the outcome. Failure means "I can't do this." Setback means "I'll do better next time."

Mindfulness

I have already mentioned this trait. The term was coined by Dr. Ellen Langer, who researched the difference in motivation and quality of work between people who did things mindlessly and people who were "mindful" in what they did. In one study, she found that elderly residents who were given the responsibility to make decisions about nurturing a plant were more active and cheerful than those who had no such project. Caring involvement and responsibility is one part of being mindful. The other concerns decreasing habitual, automatic behavior.

Sticking with routines, Langer found, not only restricts

our thinking from taking creative directions, but can also harbor behavior that is dangerous to ourselves, such as a pilot who routinely flies in warm climates, then is assigned to make a flight that takes him into icy conditions. If he automatically prepares for a routine flight, he is likely to run into trouble. Such behavior has resulted in more than one tragic plane crash.

Students can adopt automatic behavior as well. A psychology professor once walked into the room and told everyone to stand up. They all did. He asked them why. They answered, "because we were told to." He wondered why no one thought to question why they were being told to stand up in a situation where it made no sense.

Students engage in mindless behavior by merely going through the motions, following directions thoughtlessly and retaining little useful information. Often I ask students what motivates them to take my course and very few of them know. One group of students was confused by the question of what it means to be a student! This sort of mindlessness is encouraged by passive forms of education. Students are not encouraged to determine *why* they should learn something, just that they *should* learn it, and that's that.

Mindful students want to know why they are learning a particular subject, or why they are learning something in a particular way. In this way they are developing a context of meaning, priorities, and goals; they do not simply follow directions because they are told to do so.

Mindfulness is responsibility, active and informed choice, and self mastery. What mindful people say and do *matters* to them.

_____ Ability to Relax

As you will learn in the next section, the art of inner learning eludes forced effort. The relaxed mind is the most receptive mind, but receptive minds are not necessarily passive minds. You can be both alert and relaxed simultaneously, and it is just such a combination that works best for developing the state of flow and creativity that makes inner learning most productive and enjoyable. I will say more about this later.

_____ Capacity to Self-Correct

It is not easy to admit to having made a mistake, and it is even harder to actually learn from our mistakes, but the most successful people do just that. Making mistakes helps you to see where you are going wrong and to re-orient yourself. Correcting your thoughts or behavior is the step that follows reframing setbacks as challenges.

_____ Ability to be Challenged

Some of the brightest students I have ever taught share the problem of being unable to admit that their ideas, or their ways of expressing those ideas, were open to challenge. Once again, we can look to Socrates, who never felt entirely "finished" in his pursuit of truth. If you adopt an attitude of admitting that you can always improve, then challenges will not seem as much like attacks but rather opportunities to examine yourself for ways to make positive changes. The challenge, itself, may be wrong, but a positive attitude toward receiving the challenge keeps you alert and open to change. A defensive response is a weak response, exposing the possibility that you have not really thought through what you have said or done, and do not want anyone to recognize that. Keep in mind that challenge is one way to continually upgrade your personal standards.

_____ Positive Self-Esteem

Just as negative self-esteem is a hindrance to learning, positive self-esteem can enhance it. You have confidence in your abilities and project an image that inspires others to cooperate with you, improving your chances even more. If you are comfortable with yourself, others will be comfortable with you, and even be drawn toward you. What you think of yourself is up to you, although you may have to work hard at achieving a positive perspective. Setting a few small goals and achieving them will help you to feel better about yourself, and as you continue to raise your standards and make your goals progressively more difficult, you will continue to increase your self-respect.

With a positive self-esteem, you will also depend less on others' point of view, and develop expectations for yourself that originate from within. As such, you will take more pleasure in what you do because you have a sense of control and accomplishment, as well as an eagerness for the future.

Summary

Psychologists who work with "peak performers"—those whose success results from their inner drive and motivation—have made lists of the traits most often observed in such people. Those same traits occur for peak performance in learning. Although other traits, like enthusiasm and faith, may also play a role, it should be clear from this chapter the sort of core qualities that will best serve you as you move along through the next section. You may not need them all. You may already possess many of them. It should be clear by now that how well you develop the art of inner learning for yourself will depend primarily on you, both in character and in action.

Exercise

Just as you exercised self-awareness to locate your internal obstacles to learning, you will also need to know something about your strengths. Do a preliminary assessment based on the traits listed above, and add any to the list that you think are missing. You can use the descriptions from Chapter 1 for this exercise.

Summary of Part 1

- Although learning is often equated with mechanical skills, the art of being a student also involves internal dynamics.
- Approaching your education with the motivation to master the art of inner learning will make your learning experience more enjoyable and productive.
- Self-motivation is more effective than expecting motivation to come from others.
- You can motivate yourself by making it clear what learning means to you.
- Learning is a partnership between teacher and student, each with his or her own responsibilities.
- Your responsibilities include taking an active approach, setting goals, being mechanically prepared, knowing what you want, and becoming aware of how your values affect your style of thinking (thus affecting your ability to learn).
- While there are external conditions that can hinder learning, you can overcome them with sufficient motivation, mental agility, and independent thinking.
- Inner obstacles to learning may be less obvious, so you must broaden your self-awareness.
- While internal obstacles exist there are also personality traits that facilitate learning, and self-awareness can reveal those traits that can move you toward your goals.
- The art of inner learning relies on you, the student, to take the necessary steps to prepare yourself to maximize your strengths and opportunities for learning effectively and enthusiastically.

PART 2

The Art of Learning

Techniques

7

Double Reflection
and Self-Awareness

C hristopher always sat in the back of the room, arms
folded, with a glum expression on his face as he listened to the professor and other students discuss subjects
in the classroom. He looked angry. The professor avoided
drawing him into the discussion because his posture con-
veyed the message that he wished he were not there at all.
The other students never spoke to him either and it puz-
zled him. He had no idea how he was coming across
because he had never stopped to think about how others
might interpret his body language.

"The unexamined life," said Socrates, "is not worth living." It's a catchy phrase, but just what does self-examination mean? I listed self-awareness in previous chapters as
an important quality to possess, and the lack of it as a
block to learning. Clearly, Christopher could have bene-
fitted from a little self-awareness, but just how easy is it for
us to take a good look at ourselves, and of what real value
is it in the classroom?

This chapter is about learning how to recognize your
personality traits and mannerisms, both positive and negative. You were asked to do preliminary self-assessments of
your traits, but the fact is, you may not even be aware of
traits that you actually have. The method involved is not
the only one you can use, but it may offer assistance if you
are stuck. It allows you to do a self-assessment in a more

insightful manner than simply trying to observe yourself. Before describing it, let's explore the need for it.

_____ The Opaque Self

The Russian author, Dostoevsky, was once in a prison camp for political prisoners. One Easter morning, his fellow prisoners were engaged in raucous singing and gambling. Disgusted, he went for a walk. In the yard he met a Polish prisoner, who spat out, "I detest these pigs!" Dostoevsky was shocked, then realized at once that he had been thinking the same thoughts expressed in the other man's words. He saw his own attitude of superiority mirrored in the Polish man's, and he was ashamed. It had taken the other man's action to make him recognize in himself what he had been blind to until that moment. Having some aspect of ourselves blocked from our view makes self-examination a bit slippery.

Sometimes we fail, like Christopher in the opening paragraph, to see our own behavior. It is likely that we all have these blindspots. To deny it would be like denying you have a shadow behind you simply because you cannot see it. We are so close to our own feelings and behaviors that such blindness is inevitable, especially if we do not *like* certain traits that we possess. If learning means finding out what it is about our own personalities that can hinder or facilitate the process, and if those traits are somehow closed off to us, then we really do need a method of self-examination that can illuminate them to us. So while self-examination is on the list of personality strengths, it also stands out as an important bridge between us and aspects of ourselves that makes those other traits accessible.

It may seem like a tough project to begin looking for things about yourself that you cannot see very easily, and it is. Especially if you suspect that you might discover things you do not wish to face. However, before you shrug your shoulders in despair at the apparent enormity or discomfort of the task ahead, let me assure you that this method has been used with success by therapists who find it to be a valuable tool, not only with clients, but for their own growth. You will not be asked to delve as deeply into yourself as clients in therapy, but only to attempt to assess the mannerisms related to your own style of learning. You can take it as far as you want. The method is called "double reflection."

_____ Double Reflection: Context

It was Soren Kierkegaard, the nineteenth-century Danish philosopher, who coined the phrase, "double reflection." He put a name to the intuitive sense of ourselves that we all have the capacity to experience in brief, indirect flashes, as with Dostoevsky above. While it is not a phrase commonly used, the concept of double reflection is evident in many self-assessment techniques. It relies on the recognition of how our unique and personal subjective experience is part of the way we form concepts about our world.

It is first important to understand that there is no clear dividing line between our internal experience and our experience of the external world. You are already aware of how your values and moods can affect your perspective and behavior. How you view the world is influenced by how you feel. If you are depressed, you may not see the vibrant colors that spring out at you when you are happy, even though you may be looking right at them. If you've had a bad experience with a history teacher in high school, you will probably be less inclined to view a college history course with enthusiasm.

Those are simple examples, but it gets even more complicated. You also cannot observe yourself the way you observe objects or events around you. Your experience is much too complex, partly because, unlike looking at an object like a desk or a book that just sits there in front of you, your experience is continuous and you can only be aware of a small percentage of it at any given moment.

For example, a great deal is happening within your experience at this moment about which you may be unaware. While you are reading, you are also breathing, your body may be digesting something, there may be traffic or other noise nearby, there may be a draft, or it may be hot. You become aware of each of these things as I point them out, but you were probably not aware of them until then, nor can you hold them all in your mind at once. That lack of all-pervasive awareness is what makes those blindspots in your personality possible.

To get a sense of this, try for a moment to think about what you are presently thinking about. You will find that such a task becomes a matter of capturing the present moment and holding it there *while* you think about it. Yet the thought can never really be caught and held; it is already past. You cannot make it stop any more than you can use your fingers to stop a river.

That is the nature of the human mind. Consciousness cannot be fully aware of itself, for each moment of "thinking-about" is too fluid and elusive for translating into fixed thoughts or words. While you are trying to focus on making your experience clear to you by thinking about it, there is too much happening each and every moment for you to be able to capture it all. Some of it will inevitably escape your awareness. Because consciousness is this way, you can never fully observe everything about yourself.

To get a sense of this, try an experiment. Right where you are, describe in as much detail as possible the chair upon which you are sitting (or some other object accessible to you). Now do the same thing with yourself.

You should recognize the difference immediately. The chair is as static as the labels you apply to it: brown, wooden, maybe one leg too short. You, however, are not. While the words you use to describe yourself may capture *something* of what you are feeling, any description will ultimately fail to do justice to the entire range and complexity of your experiencing.

To make matters even more complex, the French philosopher, Jean Paul Sartre, reminds us that we constantly transcend ourselves—that with each moment comes a new opportunity to make decisions with respect to things about ourselves or our situations. We can remain as we are or change; and we *can* change a great deal, more so than can

a chair or a tree or a door. Our moment-to-moment existence is dynamic not static, and there is room to make
decisions about who and how you want to be. But in order
to change in a way that is *self*-empowered, you must become aware of the need for it and just what it is about
yourself that you will focus on. Although the degree of
complexity and freedom of your experience may seem confusing, it actually puts more control into your hands.

You cannot escape yourself. You are who you are. If you
fail to perceive something about yourself that can interfere
with your learning, you are the one who will be most hurt
by it. Similarly, if you fail to perceive something about
yourself that can assist you, you can also be hurt. Learn this
method of double reflection, then give it a try. You may be
pleasantly surprised, even if you discover things you don't
like, because only then will you also discover the opportunity to do something about it.

_____ Double Reflection: Content

It is one thing to say, "I know I have a few faults," and to
be able to name them. It is another thing to really *experience* them and their impact on your life. For example, you
may realize, intellectually, that you are self-absorbed or
inconsiderate, but you may not really know what this
means in your life until you lose an opportunity because of
it. *Then* you feel it!

In other words, there are two ways of knowing yourself:
thinking about who you are and really *feeling* the impact of
who you are. The second form of knowledge is more profound than the first, and makes more of an impact. Feeling
something tends to be more motivating than simply being
intellectually or mentally aware of it. Your body and mind
are more united.

The method of double reflection is about this second
form of self-knowledge. It delivers to you a fuller self-
awareness. To take note of yourself in a way that involves
your whole experience requires that you shake your reli-
ance on language in thought or speech as an exclusive

expression of your experience. Words can at best only *signal* the entire range of emotions, moods, pain, and pleasure. You will have a better grasp of double reflection if you can recognize this fact.

Think of yourself being angry or in love. How well do these words capture all that you feel? Chances are, you sense their inadequacy. The same will be true of any form of language that labels your experience. This is because your experience is both more complex and more elusive than language can capture. Just as you experienced the difference between observing yourself and observing a chair, so will you experience any form of observation and communication between yourself and things external to you as having a different experiential quality.

According to Kierkegaard, you reflect both outwardly and inwardly. "Outward reflection" is involved with making sense of your world and expressing it in words to communicate it to yourself and to others. "Inward reflection" is more intuitive and does not utilize language, but feelings and awareness. It has a stronger physical component.

The difference between these two types of reflection is similar to the difference between looking at a photograph of a river and standing next to the river. The actual experience has more dimension and is more vivid than any photograph can capture. The photograph is only a dim representation. You think about the world in which you find yourself, primarily because you need some way to capture your experience of that world, but your thoughts are not as vivid as your experience.

Because you reflect "inwardly," your experience is relative to your peculiar blend of circumstances and responses. It has a private, individual quality that makes it unique to you. Therefore, *how* you experience the world will have different qualities from the way someone else might experience it.

Think about two people approaching an exam. One person did very well on the last exam, and the second person failed. As they anticipate the exam, the first person may feel confident while the other one dreads what may happen.

Double reflection tries to get at these differences, helping each person gain a sense of how they approach an academic (or any other) situation in their own unique way. It is *not* that the exam is "objectively" both difficult and easy. It is that the same object can appear differently to different perspectives. Once you recognize that, you will not only have taken the first important step toward utilizing double reflection, but you will also become more aware of—and hopefully more tolerant of—the differences between yourself and other people.

The concept of the "inward reflection" may confuse you. This is partly due to the label Kierkegaard attached to it. You usually associate the term "reflection" with thinking. However, the inward reflection bypasses language and relies on an intuitive awareness that probes the fluid qualities of your experiencing more acutely than verbal labels allow. It gives you a sense of your own personal, concrete *presence* in the way you think about things. Your judgments and interpretations about your situations are placed into the context of your life. You can see this in the following example.

In a psychology seminar, students were assigned to read Kafka. One young man came to class clearly frustrated. As discussion centered on a difficult novel, he suddenly burst out, "The problem with Kafka is that he didn't get enough sex!"

Everyone was silent. The student blushed as he suddenly realized that he had revealed something about *himself* in his reaction, rather than about Kafka. There seemed no "objective" reason why he would come to that conclusion. We had not been examining Kafka's life. Also, no one else had read the passages in quite the way *he* had. Realizing that, he saw himself mirrored in his evaluation! Something about his own situation had influenced what he'd thought and said about Kafka that day (just as something in someone else's situation had steered that person into other ways of responding or reacting). Had he practiced a little double reflection as he read, he might have saved himself some embarrassment.

Our experience is a difficult influence to escape. It is like a man on a ship running from a storm. He has nowhere to go!

Similarly, all of us look at life from a perspective colored by our experiences. Your classroom style will inevitably be influenced by who you are. If you tend to judge people by their clothes, you might not listen to a professor who dresses poorly. If you tend to give people the benefit of the doubt, you may learn more easily than someone who does not.

Heidegger, a German philosopher, calls this condition *"befindlichkeit,"* meaning that you are always present to yourself, however inarticulately or obscurely. Take the example of driving. You are not always aware of your driving habits as you drive, but your lack of awareness does not change the fact that *you* are still guiding the wheel, pressing the gas pedal, turning with the curve of the road. You cannot escape the fact that your perspective is limited to your body, to your circumstances, to your abilities. You can see this in the different styles in which people drive. You are attuned to the world in a way that is peculiarly your own. It makes you an individual, but it also limits you to a particular perspective that is flavored by facts and events peculiar to you. And because you feel as well as think about your situation, you will be influenced by your total experience, not just by your intellectual understanding. Double reflection shows you that your mind is not detached from your body by reminding you of the personal context of your thinking—the *way* you participate in it

The difference between the two ways that we reflect, and how double reflection can be developed can be seen in the following example:

1. You are watching a television program. You are completely immersed, your face and body tense. A friend walks in and says, "Gee, you sure look tense."

2. You are watching a television program. You are completely immersed, your face and body tense. A friend comes in, walks over and mimics your face and posture.

In the first scenario, as soon as the friend mentions your

bodily posture, you become aware of it, but may fail to *feel* what it was like. The verbal label, "tense," may inform you of what your friend saw, but does not necessarily connect you to your *experience* of tension. In the second scenario, you are taken by surprise. You had been so absorbed that you did not realize what you looked like. When you saw it imitated, you felt it at once. It brought you closer to your-self than did the first approach.

The first reflection can be a product of what you might want to believe about yourself rather than what you are actually experiencing. You can deny being tense if you don't actually feel it and continue to use mental defenses to maintain self-deception. The double reflection broadens your awareness to the point where it becomes difficult to deny your experience. Double reflection puts you in touch with yourself. It plays off what you think and shows you *how* you are involved with what you think, i.e., that you thought about Kafka's novel (or any other subject) in *that* way. It shows you the *lived* expression of your thinking, not just the verbal expression of it.

The question now is, how do you learn how to practice double reflection, and what real value does it have in your education?

_____ Double Reflection: Method

Double reflection can be understood through simple techniques:

The place to begin is with your experience in the class-room. While there will be similarities to high school, there are enough differences to make the college experience a bit foreign. It is within this unfamiliarity that you can find out much about yourself.

Your initial sense of sitting in the classroom may feel awkward. Perhaps it is physically unlike anything you have experienced before. Perhaps all the new faces intimidate you. It intrudes upon your familiar world and may provoke a feeling much like homesickness or anxiety; you wish you were someplace where you are more comfortable. You are unsure how you will do, whether you will succeed, whether you are doing the right thing even by being there. The uncertainty challenges you and makes you feel self-conscious. College has made a claim on you larger than any other responsibility you have yet encountered; you are more alone with it, and there is more on the line in proving yourself. Your skills and talents are no longer taken for granted.

You will have certain reactions to this situation. *Pay attention to them.* Your reactions say much about you as an individual. It is within the gaps between you and your situation, created by discomfort, that you will get the best glimpse of your needs and values. This is how double reflection takes place. Something provokes you into *feeling* yourself *in* your situation. If you take advantage of it to examine what it is about you that creates the reactions or responses that you experience, you can then decide whether those needs and values add to or detract from your learning experience.

Sandy took a course in creative writing. She was asked to learn a technique foreign to her past experience. It involved letting go of control in order to allow the unconscious more freedom to influence her writing. The technique seemed awkward to her and she felt that her writing suffered. She became frustrated and fell into using more familiar techniques for writing, therefore blocking herself from the potential benefits of learning something new.

At that point, she realized how much she valued familiarity, security, and competence. She decided to give the new technique another try, even though it frightened her. As she concentrated on it, she lost touch with the subjects about which she was writing and realized how important it was for her to be in control. The need was hindering her from relaxing and allowing the technique to work *through* her, as the teacher intended it to do.

She had understood the tool when it was explained, but her typical confidence in intellectual comprehension had failed to prepare her for the actual experience of using the new method. She began to panic, unable to reach the point where loss of control was not threatening. She was so involved in wanting to project an air of competence that she ignored the intent behind the introduction of the new technique.

Sandy began to see that her first perception of the new approach had been too narrow and restricted. She had viewed it strictly as a matter of technical skill. That view had to change, she realized, although it was initially positive in that it helped her gain the courage to "get her feet wet." Sandy was able to use, in the gap that had opened up between herself and her writing, the quick glimpse she'd had of how she reacted to the new approach. Taking advantage of her insight into herself and her style, she was able to understand how she hindered herself and began to make some changes.

As a student, you have access both to your positive and your negative feelings about a learning situation. You can find motivating values in both. Recognize not only *what* you think about the situation (e.g., "I hate taking so many notes," "I wish the teacher would say more about the exam," "I can't understand this math; I don't know why I keep trying"), but also *how* you think, i.e., what it is about you that prompts thinking about the situation in *that* way (or *not* thinking about it in some other way). Do it soon. It is when you are most uncomfortable that your hungers and fears, reactions and responses most clearly stand out.

Another aid in seeing yourself through double reflection is to compare how you react to the way others around you react. You will find out about yourself through both similarities, as did Dostoevsky, and differences, as Sandy did.

Other students who were learning the same writing technique as Sandy reacted to it quite differently. One used it like a hammer. He felt aggressive and he adjusted the tool for his mood. Another student shuffled back and forth indecisively between feeling overpowered by the technique, and feeling guilty when he used it effectively. Yet a fourth person claimed she thoroughly disliked the tool, although the others observed that she simply felt helpless to understand it and could not admit it. How each of these students reacted or responded to the same technique reveals something of who each of them is.

I often use an exercise in my classes called guided fantasy, which I referred to earlier in another context. I ask students to imagine themselves going down a hallway until they come to a door. I then instruct them to go through the door and take the stairs. I tell them that they have come to a room which they can furnish to make it their own, in any way they like. After a few minutes, I ask them to describe their fantasy to the rest of the class.

Most people are quite surprised at how others imagined the assignment. The details are left purposely vague, so that the hallway can be long or short, dark or light. They can walk, shuffle, trot or run down it. The door may be open or closed, large or small. The stairs may go up or down, straight or circular. But it is in the room where the most divergences occur.

One student envisioned a dark, womb-like room underground with spartan furnishings. Another went upstairs to a room with a deck, and filled all the walls with a stereo system. Another had a special friend waiting for him. Yet another filled the room with statues and plants.

Try this exercise yourself with a group of friends. You can learn about yourself by seeing what you did and did not put in your room, and what you like or dislike about someone else's room. Unless you actually have the chance to compare, it is often difficult for you to see things about yourself when you furnish your room. You may simply take for granted that others will have similar tastes and similar fantasies. But they don't, and sometimes the differences can shock you into seeing a very personal side of yours.

A third means for learning double reflection is to devise a way to provoke it in a friend or roommate. We all know people who deny something about themselves so obvious that we simply shake our heads at their blindness. To get such people to see something they do not want to see is tricky.

For example, a student who does not want to see that it

is his own procrastination that results in poor grades may blame other people. If you were to point out to him that you see how it is in fact, he, himself, who is responsible, he would not only *not* listen to what you say, but would become so angry that he blocks any further attempt by you or someone else to help him. Approaching him directly only allows him to strengthen his defenses and continue to look for someone else to blame.

However, suppose you told that person a "story" about a "friend" of yours who had this same problem. Without making it obvious (this is the hard part) that you were talking about *him*, you may get him to see himself in your "story." Approaching him indirectly, without letting on that you recognize his faults, is less threatening and allows him to explore the possibilities without feeling embarrassed or defensive. This kind of technique is extremely effective in therapy. It serves as a mirror to the person whom you are addressing, but allows the person to make the discovery of themselves in private.

So the trick is to find a device which will show people to themselves without them knowing that you are trying to make a point about *them*. Once you see this work, you will begin to understand how easy it is for people to be blind to facets of their behavior or thinking. It is but a short step to recognizing your own potential for self-blindness or self-deception, and once you acknowledge that, you expand your awareness of yourself.

The Value of Double Reflection

Double reflection offers a variety of benefits for college students. Becoming aware of your strengths can aid you in persisting. Becoming aware of your psychological needs can help you to see how you might be defeating yourself. Becoming aware of your weaknesses can help you to accept them, to work with them, and to refrain from the negative consequences of self-criticism.

Double reflection can also help you become more tolerant of differences in other students. If you understand how your reactions in the classroom say something about yourself and your unique style, then you can generalize this to others. If you realize how easy it is to be blind to yourself and to view your opinion as the "objective truth," even when it's not, then you may have more sympathy for others in the same boat. The more *everyone* realizes how they each influence what they think and how they respond, the more easily you can work together in class discussions. Keep in mind that your professors, too, have perspectives influenced by their own situations.

Responding to external hindrances to learning is a good application for double reflection. It gives you a better grip on mental flexibility when you become more aware of what goes into your perspective. Changing your attitude about things like grades, poor teachers, uncomfortable classroom facilities or an incomprehensible text is more easily achieved if you are aware of yourself as the person in whom such change originates.

At any rate, to understand yourself better would rarely hinder you from learning, and the potential is there to actually help you.

 Summary

To assess your strengths and weaknesses as a student, you will need to expand your self-awareness. Double reflection is a means of gaining a sense of how your thinking is related to your personal experience, and how you may try to divorce one from the other. You can learn how to provoke a double reflection in yourself in a variety of ways, but one of the most effective ways is to identify values, psychological needs, and desires in situations in which they become prominent, e.g., being in a new situation or learning a new and difficult subject. The value of double reflection is that you can identify and begin to correct personal obstacles to learning that might otherwise remain debilitating blindspots. Like Dostoevsky, you can only change it if you are aware of it.

Exercises

Go back over your lists from the last two chapters, using as a context your assessment of your learning style from Chapter 1. Can you see how double reflection could help you to come up with more? Describe for yourself just what this technique can do for you in terms that make it personal and meaningful for you.

8

Mental Agility

Possessing self-awareness and doing something with it are two different things. It is not what you know but what you do with what you know that counts. You can use double reflection to gain a better sense of yourself as a learner, but at the same time, you must develop the skills that you will need to participate even more fully in the art of inner learning. The exercises in turn can assist you further with double reflection and self-assessment, like writing one paper that can be applied to two courses.

In Chapter 2, you were initially introduced to the experience of seeing more than one perspective on an idea or situation. It is time to expand on that concept by progressing from mental flexibility to mental agility: from recognizing the ambiguity of appearances to using that information so as to benefit you in your approach to learning. It is an essential step in the art of inner learning. Let us back up and explore the notion that there are many sides to a situation, keeping in mind that the one you believe is "right" may have to yield to a different one.

_____ Appearances

Have you ever felt certain you knew something only to discover that what you thought you had "known" was really something else altogether? I was walking the other day and saw my neighbor in the distance. I walked toward him. The closer I came, the less certain I felt, until finally it became clear that not only was the man in the distance *not* my neighbor, but bore no physical resemblance to him. In fact, the other person walking toward me was a woman!

It is a common experience to be mistaken in what we think we know. There are many reasons for this:

1. Our senses deceive us. Go put a straight stick in a glass of water. It will appear to be bent. If you take it out, it is clearly straight. What your eyes tell you is misleading. Or put your left hand into a bucket of hot water and your right hand into a bucket of cold water. Then stick them both into a bucket of warm water. The same water will feel both cool and warm to you, although that seems to the logical mind to be a contradiction. These common science experiments demonstrate how the senses can be tricked.

2. Our memories deceive us. Try to recall an event in which you made a fool of yourself, or made some kind of mistake, then ask someone else to relate to you the details. Compare how your memory of the situation differs from theirs. Imagine how someone who disliked you might tell the story! Whose memory is the "correct" one?

3. Information presented factually is often incomplete or not as authoritative as it had been made to sound. Listen to two different news programs on the same story, or read two news magazines or newspapers with different political slants. For example, a president raises taxes. If the publication tends to favor him, they may cast his actions in a favorable light, while another publication will find ways to make him look bad. Who would be the most authoritative source?

Or imagine someone telling you that thirty percent of all date-rape cases go unreported. If they are "unreported," how would this person know? At best, the information is speculative, but often it is presented as fact, then passed on to others to the point where it is accepted as fact. Stepping back from the way a perspective is presented can give you the insight to see what it really is.

This potential for mistake and for changing perceptions is one reason why Plato insisted that true knowledge cannot be based on perception, or on information we piece together blindly. He thought it was impossible to *know* something one day (e.g., the fact that stress causes ulcers), then *not* know it the next day because what we claim to know has changed (it is no longer clear that stress causes ulcers). Knowledge, for Plato, had to be based on something completely unchangeable if it were to be counted as knowledge at all. That is why he dismissed appearance as the basis for any sort of knowledge.

The problem with Plato's standard is that much of the information we use to give us direction in our day-to-day existence is based on the *appearance* of things. We *depend* on knowing by appearance. Often we need to make important decisions and form impressions strictly on what we perceive—the fin slicing through the water appears to be a dolphin and not a shark, or vice versa; or that a professor seems to be competent in the brief period of time you are given to decide whether to stay in a course.

But we must be careful. Even if we do not want to accept Plato's high standards for knowledge, we can still make mistakes that would fail to pass even our own, more practical standards. Appearances not only can deceive us, but can also limit us in our pursuit of knowledge or learning. If you believe that what you see is what you know, you may not look beyond, like deciding against reading a book because you dislike the artwork on the cover. Our cultural emphasis on paying more attention to the physical senses, even if they are not one hundred percent reliable, than to other ways of knowing, like intuition, has added weight to this dependence and has thus increased the potential for narrowing our vision.

The problem with appearances is that, if it is possible to be deceived, then we may be prone to being tricked by *any* appearance, so how can we tell when we are and when we are not being deceived? It is easy to tell with the stick in the glass of water, but not all situations are so readily resolved. It may seem safe to believe those assumptions based on appearances that everyone else agrees with than to try out something new. Safety in numbers is often translated as "truth." However, this is a symptom of mental rigidity and mindlessness—not a goal in the art of inner learning.

The very fact that appearances can be deceiving means

they are ambiguous: they can mean more than one thing. Such deception can be either negative or positive. While we tend to think of being deceived as being made to take a position inferior to what we thought we had with regard to the knowledge we possess, it can also have the opposite effect. If our perception of something makes it less than it actually is, then getting past the appearance and seeing that we were wrong can actually be beneficial. Mental flexibility gives us this insight. Mental agility means we go ahead and discover the benefits.

_____ Seeing Beyond Appearances

In an earlier chapter, I discuss how the pilot in the story, *The Little Prince,* had landed his disabled plane in the desert and had discovered a little man claiming to be a prince from another planet. Imagine how you would react to such a discovery. In this story, we find several insightful metaphors about how too much focus on appearance— especially appearance that is reinforced by tradition or popular opinion—can be a stumbling block in our search for truths to live by, and thus how focusing on appearance can become a serious hindrance to learning.

By all appearances, the prince was just a deluded midget. However his confident manner interested the pilot, so they continued to talk. The prince asked the pilot to draw him a sheep. He had need of a sheep, he claimed, to eat the destructive "baobabs" on his planet before they took over and killed his beloved rose. The pilot drew for him several pictures. He was dissatisfied with each picture, so the pilot finally just drew a box with three tiny breathing holes, and said the sheep was inside. To his surprise, the prince peered at the picture of the box and claimed he could see the sheep, and that it had gone to sleep. It was the pilot's first lesson in looking beyond the superficial. What to him had been nothing but a drawing of an ordinary box had become, for the prince, a prized possession.

Relating this to college life, you too, must see beyond

appearances. If you tend to equate writing on the board with competence, for example, then you may be frustrated when you sign up for a course with a "board-writer" who is actually disorganized and unclear. On the other hand, if you dismiss as incompetent a professor who does not write on the board, you may miss out on learning from a very talented individual. There are many more applications for this principle. Think of one, yourself, before you go on.

In *The Little Prince,* the pilot recalled hearing about a Turkish astronomer who had discovered a planet that he named Asteroid B-16. However, because he wore a Turkish costume, the astronomer was laughed out of the International Astronomical Congress. It was only after he changed to European clothing, which was worn by everyone else at the conference, that his presentation about Asteroid B-16 was accepted; yet his presentation was precisely the same one he gave while wearing his Turkish attire!

Most of us have been guilty at one time or another of dismissing someone because of their appearance. The same holds true of dismissing a new approach to learning, simply because it is not "dressed" like those with which you are familiar.

The little prince, himself, and to his peril, had once fallen into the trap of being deceived by appearances. Before meeting the pilot, he had made the acquaintance of a snake. Because the snake was no bigger than a finger, he assumed that it was relatively harmless. "You are not very powerful," he told the snake. "You haven't even any feet." The snake protested that he was more powerful than the finger of any king: "Whomever I touch, I send back to the earth from whence he came." Despite the *appearance* of having no significance, the snake had the ability to kill with its venom. Underestimating its power could be fatal. The prince was forced to become more flexible in his judgments.

In Chapter 4, I referred to the pilot's dilemma: his plane was broken and he had run out of water. To the pilot, the desert was a threatening place. The heat and dryness were about to annihilate him. Yet the prince insisted that the desert was beautiful. He suggested that they walk out and look for a well. The pilot reluctantly agreed. He was getting nowhere with his plane. Still, he was afraid. They could die out there.

They walked for hours. The prince tired and sat down, yet continued to insist that the desert was beautiful, and what gave it its beauty was something they were *unable to see:* that perhaps it hid a well. At daybreak, they found the well. Not only had the discovery saved his life, but it had taught him the value—even the *necessity*—of looking *beyond* initial appearances. It is a lesson which you, as a student, must also learn if you are to gain the most from your education.

For example, when students prejudge how they want a course to be structured, they can shut themselves off from learning opportunities. A professor once taught a contemporary ethics course by first teaching the principles of proper argumentation so students could apply what they learned to the issues. Several students complained that the course was supposed to give them opportunities to debate with each other over the issues. They did not see the point of what the professor was showing them because they believed that logic was a completely different subject. In other words, they wanted to just argue from their opinions without learning the discipline of arguing *correctly!* What they *wanted* to do in the course prevented them from seeing the value of what was actually being taught, which would have done more for their thinking about issues than a semester's worth of gut-level, emotional debate. The course they had wanted would have allowed them to leave with the same poorly formed opinions with which they had entered. They were not willing to be flexible enough to envision another way to do things.

Such students are like the pilot, not trusting that there might be a well in the desert, simply because they trust their own judgment too much, or are afraid to take a risk on trying something new. Just as the pilot's judgment had been too heavily influenced by appearances, which he strongly believed, and not nurtured enough in the sort of *vision* that comes with mental flexibility, so, too, can the judgment of the student be similarly underfed. It is not always the case that a course taught be an atypical format will be superior, but the potential is there for students to still learn something that they had not anticipated. However, they can only find the "well" if they are at least open to the possibility, then make up their minds to go ahead and search for it. If they decide to remain near a "defunct plane" in hopes that something in their circumstances will change, they may "die of thirst."

_____ Going Beyond Appearances

Try this puzzle. Harry is in a prison with concrete walls that extend several feet into the ground. The doors are impenetrable. The floor is made of packed earth. Eight feet overhead is a skylight, but there is nothing in the room to climb upon. Harry is only six feet tall—too short to reach it. Yet he escaped by digging a hole and going through the skylight! How?

The problem may seem puzzling at first. The ceiling is above, the floor below. How can he dig *down* to escape through the skylight?

The answer is actually obvious, although you may not have seen it right away. Harry dug a hole in order to pile up dirt until he was able to reach the skylight! To "get" this, you have to liberate your mind from the images suggested by the wording of the puzzle. That is the key to mental agility.

In the following chapters, I am going to ask you to liberate yourself in a similar manner. I want you to substitute one appearance with another: the appearance that the traditional approach to education is the best way to learn vs. the appearance that the experience of "flow" and the development of inner instruction is the best way to learn. Then I will ask you to move beyond the appearance to see the potential for yourself.

If it is true that you can be deceived by appearance, then

you can be deceived by either of these approaches. However, research has shown that the "tradition" has become somewhat ineffective. Focus on the mechanics of learning—to the neglect of the inner person—has encouraged in some places an "assembly line" approach to education. Students feel that they become faceless consumers, especially at large universities, rather than unique individuals.

The appearance that traditional approaches to learning are "right" simply because they have been accepted for a long time can make other approaches seem "wrong," even though they are merely *different.* You can be deceived by this. You can also be deceived by the appearance that another approach can offer you something more. The important thing to do is to develop vision to see beyond *both* appearances to possibilities not immediately apparent. This may lead you into a desert where there is no well, or you may be refreshed in ways that you had never anticipated. Only if you act will you find out.

I have already mentioned the student who refused to imagine other possible scenarios for reality because he grasped so desperately at the security of views influenced by an empirical framework. In contrast, a classmate, Kevin, was willing to explore the possibilities and enjoyed the course a great deal more. Kevin did not require the same mental anchoring and was able to experience views different than his own by detaching himself temporarily from his ego needs and recognizing that there *were* more ways than one to see "reality." For him, the exercise of imagining himself as a brain in a vat being stimulated by sensory electrodes, or trying to prove he was not dreaming, was not only fun, but provoked further scenarios that gave him the imaginative flexibility he needed to understand reality structures different from his own. As a result, he also developed an appreciation for other cultures that view reality differently from ours. He not only learned some of the slippery subtleties of a philosophy course, but he also found new interests, leaving his more timid and rigid classmate behind in Plato's cave.

Looking beyond appearances requires faith, as it did for

the pilot. There are no guarantees. However, to cling onto something merely for the sake of security or because it is "accepted" may not only prevent you from getting the most from your education, but may even strip you of real enjoyment in the learning process. To "find the well" requires imagination and vision. Vision comes from flexibility. Having both, along with the willingness to go beyond appearances, increases your mental agility.

_____ Summary

Each of us is vulnerable to making false assumptions based on appearances, which then prevents us from seeing beyond those appearances. We are like the pilot in some ways. Yet, if we keep in mind the well in the desert, the snake, the sheep in the box, and the Turkish astronomer, we might develop the flexibility of mind that we need to allow ourselves to be educated beyond our own expectations. Mental flexibility provides the initial momentum.

To get involved with skills that move us toward the art of inner learning, we also need vision. We must be prepared to practice the steps outlined thus far, or risk deriving nothing but "head" knowledge from the rest of this book. The benefits of inner learning will be evident not only in the quality of the course work done, but also in quality experience. We must exercise the faith that may be necessary to try something new, in order to reap the full enjoyment of learning in this manner.

The next four chapters provide the tools, and the last chapter in this section describes the experience.

Exercises _____

The following exercises are designed to help you improve your mental flexibility:

1. Look at this symbol. What is it?

Now come up with something else, and keep thinking until you have made a list of at least five things it could be.

2. Think of as many uses as you can for a fork. Do the same with some subject you are studying.

3. Think up a new way for taking notes in class that you have never before tried.

4. Decide what changes you would make in one of your classrooms to make a better design for effective learning.

9

Visualization

Kim had a final exam coming up. He knew that if he did not do well on this exam, he might flunk the course, and if he flunked the course, he would not graduate. The pressure of what the test signified weighed heavily on his mind as he prepared to study. He began to think of the consequences of failing, and the scenarios he envisioned prevented him from studying effectively.

Finally, he closed the books and concentrated on replacing negative imagery with positive. He used his imagination to "see" himself seated at his desk in the classroom, alert, relaxed, assured. While he breathed deeply, he thought about what the classroom smelled like, what it looked like, where he sat in relation to other students, in relation to the professor, what he would wear. In short, he put himself as vividly as possible into the position of taking the exam, then used his resources to call up a positive, confident image.

Over the next several days, Kim rehearsed this image to the point that he sincerely believed he would do well. When he studied, he felt less stressed and more relaxed, using the image to guide and motivate him. When he actually arrived at the classroom on the day of the exam, he felt better than he thought possible. He defeated his test anxiety, and as a result, he was free from the burdens of tension. His mind was less likely to be blocked and more likely to have access to the material he studied. His performance was a genuine reflection of what he had studied, rather than a mirror of his fears.

"When you imagine yourself doing something in a certain way," say psychologists Bernie Zilbergeld and Arnold

Lazarus, "the mind tends to take this as a real experience." Studies on imagery in sports show that the muscles, respiratory, and nervous systems respond as strongly to visualizing an event as they do to experiencing the event, itself. If this is the case, then visualizing yourself in your classroom situation and teaching yourself to relax will prepare your body to respond in a similar way when you actually arrive at that location. Imagery can be a powerful technique.

Although Kim was able to use imagery to improve his chances for a better grade, he might have done better had he looked beyond the grade, and even beyond the course, to tap the power of imagery to become more involved and effective in the process of *learning*. This chapter will focus on using the technique of visualization as a tool for greater self-control in developing the art of inner learning.

Where Images Originate

Dr. Roger Sperry and Dr. Robert Ornstein are the names most often associated with the theory that the brain operates by a dual system of processing conscious and unconscious activities. Our perceptions, skills, and abilities are influenced by the side of the brain that we tend to favor, and this preference is often culturally influenced, by placing higher values on certain functions than on others.

Although it is controversial that the functions are so clearly divided between the halves of the brain, the left side has been credited with qualities related to being linear, sequential, logical, analytical, rational and language-oriented. The right side seems to evoke imagery, patterns, spatial structure, holistic problem-solving, rhythm, emotions, synthesis, intuition, spontaneity and insight. Whether these divisions are actually accurate may be debatable. Nevertheless, the dual-brain theory provides us with an accessible (and acceptable) framework for developing ways to access our capacity to imagine.

Imagery has been identified as a "right-brain" function. It has suffered from neglect in our rational, language-oriented culture, and as a result, few students know its power or how to tap it. Oftentimes the resources of the right brain are filtered through fear and anxiety rather than through confidence and affirmation. Imagery can be either positive or negative. How we use the right brain depends on how we understand its power in our lives, and how that power can be channeled and controlled.

We tend to rely on words to represent our experiences to ourselves and to others. Sometimes language is adequate for this kind of expression, but other times it does not quite capture what we actually feel or what we wish to express, as pointed out in the discussion of double reflection. Sometimes words *fragment* rather than represent an experience. Because imagery goes beyond words, it can help you become more attuned to the wholeness and integrity of your thoughts and feelings. It can also give you the power to influence your own future.

Visualization Methods

Although the words "visualization" and "imagery" suggest mental *pictures*, the method of putting yourself mentally into a situation involves a wealth of details, including imagining noises, smells, and bodily sensations. The more vivid and more full-dimensional an image is, the more effectively it will work for your goals. A report from the National Research Council in 1988 showed that the use of repetitive visualization, called "mental rehearsal," resulted in genuine gains in learning performance.

To use imagery as a *technique* is to control how you think and feel about a situation, to help you achieve your goals, and to assist you in tapping your potential for self-fulfillment. You want to move away from negative images of anger, weakness, or failure, and toward positive, empowering images, with an ultimate goal of improving your *self* image in response to challenges. You can practice imagery almost anywhere as a way to control your responses and improve your performance or enhance your experience.

There are two basic steps: learning how to visualize and practicing it.

The first requirement for learning how to visualize is to relax. You should begin by making it easy for yourself. Focus on simple situations, like building up courage to talk with a professor, or diminishing anxiety about raising your hand to ask a question in class. Use Kevin's method above as a model, filling your images with specific detail.

While you can practice anywhere, it is best to learn the skill in a distraction-free atmosphere. Dress comfortably and sit in a comfortable position, but do not become so comfortable that you're in danger of falling asleep. Breathe deeply several times, clearing your mind of all distractions.

Think about the situation you want to work on, and try to imagine yourself there. You can either watch yourself perform or you can watch the situation as if you were actually experiencing it. The latter is more effective, but the former may be less threatening. Concentrate on the immediate details. What are you wearing? If there are other people involved, what do they look like? What are their facial expressions and body postures? What are they doing? What are you doing? How do your feel? Are there any sounds or smells? What does your mouth feel like? What are you feeling emotionally?

Stay focused on this situation as you tighten then relax your muscles several times to encourage continued relaxation.

If your image becomes upsetting, leave it and focus on something that soothes you, like a deserted ocean beach or a garden. Go over your body, part by part, starting with your toes, and concentrate on relaxing each part, breathing deeply all the while. When you feel relaxed, return to your original image.

When you are able to stay with the immediate details of the situation, think about what you want to achieve with this visualization. Are you trying to get over a fear? To improve your performance? To reduce stress? To master a skill? To change your response? To see what it would be like to succeed? Or just to feel better? You must be able to spell out for yourself how you want to change an experience or situation in order to alter your imagery toward success. The more specific you can be, the more easy it will be to envision the details and the less prone you will be to distractions.

When you know your goal, begin to move toward it until you see yourself achieving it. Sometimes it helps to say out loud, "I am succeeding at _____," or "I am able to achieve _____." If the goal involves several steps, imagine yourself taking and succeeding at each step. Do not skip any steps in your eagerness to see yourself at the end. Imagery is most effective if you can take yourself through all the motions.

Visualization is a form of self-hypnosis. You are talking yourself into taking a new perspective on the future that can ensure that your actions produce, as closely as possible, the desired effect. You are in control of the content and intensity of your images, and of their direction. If you don't *feel* in control, then you must continue to work on the process until you do.

It may take you awhile, but keep working until the imagery is quite vivid to you. Anyone can achieve this, although it comes more quickly to some than to others. When you feel you have mastered the technique of placing yourself in a situation and succeeding with your goals for that situation, move on to more complex situations, like learning how to improve your concentration or mastering a difficult subject.

Once you have developed your vision to the point that it is working the way you want it to—to change your attitudes, perspective, emotion, or performance—you can strengthen its effect by going through all the steps again, and then again. This is called mental rehearsal. Your mind gets so used to the image that it accepts it as the real experience. The process is like what actors do to get ready for a part—play the part over and over. The more they practice, the more skilled and competent they become. The same thing will happen for you.

You can utilize past successes to help you to envision success for the future. You can use symbols to help you to realize your goal. For example, if you want to gain more control over your situation, see yourself as a powerful animal, or enlarge your hand to get a good, hard grip on things. Use a person you admire to be a model for what you want to see yourself doing. If you have trouble getting comfortable, imagine yourself as your favorite movie actor, or a character from a novel with whom you identify, doing what you want to do. Move from the passive receptivity of the first step to actively choosing and controlling your scenario. There is no limit to what you can do to assist your imagination to work for you. After all, it is *your* imagination!

To give you an example of how this can work, read what happened to Nancy. She imagined herself as having few ideas worth expressing. Whenever she thought about saying something in class, she cringed at the vision of other students looking at her as if she were stupid. When she was introduced to the concept of visualization, she could hardly progress past the first step, because putting herself in the situation inevitably spelled ridicule. Yet she persisted—as initially painful as it was—and was able to envision one friendly face in the crowd. She told her idea to that imaginary person and felt encouraged by the smile she "saw." Then she imagined two friendly faces, then three, until she was able to feel somewhat comfortable with the idea of actually expressing herself in a real classroom. She had to rehearse this visualization over and over, but eventually she did participate in discussion and was pleased to discover that no one ridiculed her.

In another class, she was assigned a five-minute speech. Normally the idea would have terrified her and she might even have dropped the course. However, once she had experienced the success of her visualization, she felt she could put it to use to get over her fear of speaking in class. She followed the same steps, rehearsing her speech over and over in front of an imaginary class until she was able to actually do it. She was nervous, but not frightened, and when it was over and she realized that she could actually *do* something like that, it gave her confidence for the future.

The Uses of Imagery

Visualization techniques have been implemented in many fields, such as art, business, and sports. Students can tap into this technique as well because there are many possible applications in college. The list below is not exhaustive but will give you a sense of the broad range of uses.

To set goals

One of the traits of a successful person is the ability to set goals. It is important that you begin setting both *process* goals and *final* goals. Sometimes it is easier to set the process goals if you can actually envision what it will take to achieve your final goals. It may also be easier to set those final goals if you can envision yourself accomplishing them. You may also discover which of your goals is unrealistic if you *cannot* see yourself accomplishing them.

To solve problems and make decisions

There are many strategies available for solving problems ranging from those found in textbooks to personal situations. Any of the strategies can be enhanced with visualization. Using images makes more vivid both the situation and the steps that need to be taken to solve the problems or make the decisions.

With problem-solving, you usually have to find ways to break the problem down. With decision-making, you must be able to project into the future and determine the outcome for the various courses of action upon which you must decide. Putting yourself fully into hypothetical situations will enable you to see what needs to be done, or what must be avoided; the more vividly you can do that, the more readily you can take appropriate action.

To reduce stress

Visualization works as well with changing your emotional responses as it does with helping you to set goals or solve problems. Go through the same steps, only concentrate more on how the situation *feels* rather than what it looks or sounds like. You can bring your physical response under control and change it by changing your response to those aspects of the situation that create stress. Sometimes it helps to go ahead and imagine the worst possible scenario, then imagine yourself living with it. That can reduce your fear. In other circumstances, it may be your attitude that needs to change. If, for example, stress results from your belief that you have to be perfect, you may want to rethink this self-imposed requirement and find one that is easier to live with. Visualization can aid you in discovering this, especially when it is coupled with double reflection, and in seeing how emotions change with simple alterations in the way you think.

To improve performance

You may, for example, be experiencing problem areas in your classroom performance. Perhaps you suffer from poor concentration or the inability to listen. Perhaps you cannot organize or focus your writing. Perhaps you are afraid to speak in front of a class. Perhaps you have a poor memory. With visualization, you not only can assist yourself with these areas, but you can also improve your strengths by *seeing* yourself becoming more skilled and competent.

For example, you may have trouble with listening. That's a tough one because imagining a certain bodily posture associated with alertness and concentration does not necessarily deliver to you what you need. You can switch to a metaphor. Imagine yourself as a thirsty person and the lecturer has the directions to the nearest source of water. You will have to pay close attention to get what you need. Using such a metaphor can give you a better feel for the *connection* between yourself and the material. Then, of course, you have to practice this in actual settings, because visualization is most effective when supported by your behavior.

To develop and practice flexibility

You understand that it is important to be able to see from a variety of perspectives, but it is difficult for you to do that. Visualization can help.

You can create perspective-changing exercises for your-self, like imagining all the possible uses for a familiar object. In the classroom, you can try to imagine what the situation looks like from the professor's perspective. Really try to feel what that must be like. Look around at the faces and imagine yourself standing in front of them, talking. Are they responsive? How would you feel if they were not? What would it be like to have *you* as a student? Then select someone else in the class—perhaps someone who irritates you—and imagine the classroom through that person's eyes. I have seen dramatic changes in the degree of involve-ment with students who take the time to do this sort of exercise.

You can practice this kind of exercise in almost any situation to increase your mental flexibility. Taking it a step further into behavior aids your mental agility.

To raise energy levels

Energy is a key factor in how well you perform, but there are many factors in college that contribute to depleting your energy, especially during exam periods or when many assignments are due at once. You can actually increase your energy by taking the time to imagine yourself as having more, because research shows that visualization can put you in touch with your physical energy sources. One way to do this is to imagine yourself experiencing enthusiasm for what you are doing. Another way is to breathe deeply while you visualize doing a project that needs to be done. Of course, if you neglect to eat, sleep, and get proper exercise, you cannot force water from a stone, but there are ways to use visualization to tap the energy that *is* there.

To motivate yourself

In college, you will be faced with things that you do not want to do. Rather than putting off a disagreeable or fright-ening assignment, envision yourself actually *doing* it. Go through the motions in your imagination. You'll be sur-prised at how much easier it will be to actually get to work and get the assignment done. Visualize yourself enjoying it, and increase your chances that you *will!*

You may also want to motivate yourself to do something that you *do* want to do, but that you want to do better. You can use images to help you to discover ways to achieve this goal. For example, focus on your career goals and imagine the classroom as your training ground.

To master a skill and enhance the quality of your experience

Although mastering a skill comes under the heading of improving your performance, I want to emphasize that, in this book, the technique of visualization has a larger purpose: to give you the means to master the skill of inner learning. Keep this in mind as you read the chapters on concentration, flow, and creativity. Each of these skills and experiences can be more easily mastered and enhanced if you use the technique of visualization to take yourself through the steps.

Visualization as a tool is not necessarily connected with inner learning. It can be practiced apart from that, and inner learning does not require the ability to visualize. However, each enhances the other when used in a complementary fashion, and in conjunction with the next skill, inner direction.

Exercising the Right Brain

There are several books on the market dedicated to the subject of right-brain exercise methods and you should be made aware that the following list of approaches is only a brief collection of what can be done. Nevertheless, this list calls your attention to the idea of balancing values and skills for a broader application to learning. There is some controversy over whether these exercises actually have a direct impact on learning; but they certainly strengthen mental flexibility and agility, and thus influence learning skills in a positive way, even if indirectly.

We tend to prefer approaching situations with "left-brain" strategies such as thought analysis and logic. Although you may be convinced that visualization is beneficial, you may have trouble actually practicing it, especially as a routine, or in an immediately pressing situation. There are ways, however, to get yourself more involved with "right brain" approaches.

Brain switching

One way to prevent excessive emphasis on a "half-brain" orientation is to consciously work through a range of perspectives that rely on both approaches. Understand what each approach involves and make sure you balance it with something from the other one. For example, a right-brain approach helps you to perceive the various forms involved in an optical illusion. After you identify them, analyze how you did it. Watch a movie or read a book that moves you, then articulate the essence of that emotional connection.

In the other direction, after you have gone through the steps of a logically-structured argument, think about the emotions involved. Did the argument excite you? Make you angry? Think about a discussion or a situation in which you solved a problem and an insight seemed to pop out and surprise you. This is an example of brain switching.

The idea is to bring the values associated with both perspectives into play in order to achieve a balance and get the most from your "brain" potential.

Relaxation

Relaxation can put you in touch with many capacities of your brain, including energy, and makes the process more accessible than a stressed or rigid mind. As you relax, think through any situation from perspectives that utilize qualities of both analytic and holistic orientations.

Revaluing

Sometimes people are afraid to move away from an approach they are used to, partly because they feel that taking a new direction may reduce their skill or capacity in their former approach. This is a "hydraulic" model of human functioning: they believe that to turn on the faucet in the kitchen reduces the water flow in the bathroom. However, research has shown that, not only is there no negative effect to logical and linguistic abilities when increasing your capacity to experience your right-brain potential, but all areas of mental functioning actually improve. Our tendency to prefer one side to the other—or one set of values to the other—may be depriving us of the potential for much greater benefits that come with balancing them and developing both.

Although as a society, we tend to value the left-brain capacity more than the right, you can form your own decisions about it. Giving credibility to what the right brain offers can make you more willing to acknowledge its value in your perspectives, thoughts, and actions.

Style reversal

Your style reflects your preferences. If you tend toward logic and debate, try freeing yourself long enough to become less involved in "head" strategies and more involved in an emotional experience. If you are a listener, try talking more. If you tend to agree, try disagreeing more. If you prefer to think in images, try working with logical formulas. Find a style that is quite different from the one you normally adopt in the way you react and respond to an academic situation. Chances are, this style will use more energy from the half of the brain that your preferred style neglects. This exercise provides you with mental flexibility *and* agility, both of which can be enhanced with visualization.

_____ Summary

Visual images are representations in your mind of experiences or situations, past, present, or future. They can be negative or positive and they can affect what you think and do, and how well you perform in college. You can take steps to change your negative images into positive ones, and to create scenarios that will help you to get past frustrating, frightening, or stressful situations. You can also use visualization to enhance your college experience and to help you to master skills, broaden your perspectives, and give you the greater mental agility needed for practicing the art of inner learning.

Exercises _____

1. Use visualization to work on your goals from Chapter 1. Start with a daily schedule, then go to a weekly, monthly, semester, and college plan.

2. Select a situation or skill that you want to improve and work on it with imagery and mental rehearsal. Keep track of the phases of your experience until you feel that you can use visualization techniques well enough to apply to other situations and skills.

10
Inner Direction

Richard Dotson, a pitcher for the New York Yankees, was put on the disabled list one summer to "work on his mechanics." His performance failed to improve until he decided to forget the mechanics and just go out and pitch the ball. That game was his best showing in months.

"It got to the point," he said, "where I was thinking too much before I threw a pitch. It's tough enough...without worrying about whether your leg is in the right position."

Dotson was practicing "inner direction," trusting his mind and body to work together to follow through on a procedure which both already "know," rather than *telling* himself what to do with a list of verbal instructions. Clearly, he needed to be mechanically prepared, but too much *focus* on those mechanics only hindered his performance. He had lost some of his edge because he was thinking through the mechanics in piecemeal, step-by-step fashion.

Students experience a similar situation. Too much attention to external mechanics and rules can dull rather than sharpen the mind. The art of inner learning depends on the ability to let go of these mechanics once they are mastered and to trust your mind and body to work together to apply them toward learning a subject without having to keep the mechanics consciously in mind. Visualization and double reflection put you in touch with the *whole* experience, and that experience is what I will call "inner direction."

If you reduce learning to the mechanics, it may seem natural to you to focus on such things as grades, memorization, and performance to assure yourself that you are, indeed, learning. However, you make yourself vulnerable to becoming such a slave to the mechanics that you cannot transcend them enough to allow your mind to achieve its own learning potential. Inner direction can help you to transcend.

Mechanics: External Pressures

Mike was grade-conscious. He learned that to get the best grade in a course, he had to do well on each assignment. To do well, he had to know exactly what was required for each assignment. When he read the text or took notes in class, it was always with attention to the likelihood that some particular item would be on an exam. If it sounded like the professor was talking on a tangent, Mike would raise his hand and ask, "Will this be on the test?" If it was not, he stopped viewing the information as important, even if the "tangential" information was stimulating or instructive.

Mike was so obsessed with keeping track of potential "test items" that his learning amounted to a short-term retention of material. He had a sharp mind and was able to achieve his goal of getting the highest grades, but the pattern of superficial attention and memorization tripped him up when it came to excelling in his post-graduate career, where a different type of learning habit was required. So engrossed with meeting external demands, Mike failed to develop the internal skills of attending to information that would give him the mental flexibility of moving from one situation to another.

Mike also confused good grades with genuine learning. Part of his confusion was due to the way the system is set up. Professors or parents often say that the student with the highest grade learned the most. Such is not always the case. "Average" students can demonstrate a more profound grasp of a subject than their "superior" counterparts, simply because they were interested enough in the subject to learn it for its own value, and demonstrated this in ways not measured by the grading system.

The grading system allows us to believe that learning is

taking place when, in fact, there may be nothing more happening than various levels of ability to memorize. I have already mentioned Robert M. Pirsig's book, *Zen and the Art of Motorcycle Maintenance* (a metaphor of self-awareness and the achievement of inner peace). He tried to get students to work without grades. At first they were frightened and irritated. Then they got involved in learning the subject as they had never been involved before, and turned in papers that exceeded their original performances. Removing the grades, the professor felt, forced the students to wonder each day whether they were *really* learning anything. They had no reassuring external cues. They had to concentrate on what was being taught and what their own goals were. Although many of the students still preferred the grading system, Pirsig found that the majority of those were students who did not want to motivate themselves and needed external signals to indicate that they were getting by. "The removal of grades," he said, "exposes a huge and frightening vacuum."

That vacuum can be filled by students, themselves. Mike, the grade-conscious student, never experienced the kind of concentration that originates with a person's internal motivations. He knew only how to work within a system of external rewards and punishments. In other words, he did not know how to *trust* himself in this context. But what does such trust involve?

Try an experiment. Fill a bucket or bowl full of water, almost to the brim. Now carry it across the room and back (or outside in the yard). First carry it with your eyes trained right on the bucket, telling yourself not to spill any. Chances are, if you don't spill any, you'll come very close, and the exercise will exhaust you from the strain of trying.

Now carry the bucket without looking at it. Just decide that you will carry it from point A to point B without spilling it. Then do it. If you send a mental message to your body to perform, then allow it to take over and perform in its own way, you won't spill a drop. When you don't try so hard to consciously *control* the operation, it requries much less effort to get the job done. You mentally convey to your body what you want and trust it to follow through. (Of course, you need to possess a body that *can* do the task). When you attempt to control it with too much verbal instruction, you throw off the balance of mental/physical concentration.

The student's situation is similar. We have all been trained for a long time to *try* to concentrate or to *try* to do well, rather than letting go of the "trying" part and just *doing* it. Along with that training comes self-criticism to whip us back on track should we let up, to keep us *out* of the body and into the mind. We locate learning "in the mind" and believe the body to be a distraction. And certainly it *can* be if we allow it to get sluggish, sick, or fatigued.

However, the body plays as much a part in the art of inner learning as it does in work or sport. It supplies the energy and health necessary to keep the mind alert and motivation continuous. To divide one from the other robs you of the strength gained from coordination of the two. The union of mind and body in the process of learning is greater than the sum of its parts, and even greater than either part working alone.

In the experiment with the bucket of water, it is focusing on the *bucket* that interrupts your natural balance and coordination. When you simply allow your body to do the work, it performs—sometimes in spite of you. Likewise, your mind can perform in the classroom, often beyond your own expectations, if only you will let it do what it needs to do, in chorus with your body. But first you must understand, like Dotson did, how to get beyond mechanics to sheer quality of performance.

_____ Mechanics: Self-Instruction

We often try to make ourselves learn, first by telling ourselves exactly what to do; second, by chastising ourselves when we fail to do it right, or well enough. We *force* the learning process and often end up learning much less, and enjoying it much less, than we could. Then, if we fail to accomplish what we verbally tell ourselves, we criticize.

Mike continually told himself what he needed to do. Pay attention, take good notes, read the text, figure out what might be on the test. If he did not do as well as he thought he should have on an exam, he would berate himself for not following his own instructions. He punished himself into polishing his performance, and as a result, learning was not very pleasurable or interesting. Mike had his eye set only on the goal of the grade. If he received a lower grade than he desired on a paper, he fought for the higher grade merely for the sake of having it, and never bothered to read the comments intended to help him.

We often play both the role of parent and child. We instruct, we follow the instruction, and then we reward or punish ourselves. These roles are too much for one person to assume. They contradict one another and soon lead to a confusion of identities.

It is difficult, however, to break the cycle. Our conscious instructing/criticizing mind is active and does not want to lose its control. We set goals but then cannot relax and allow ourselves to get to them, so we lose out on enjoying the process. The goals then become standards of *measurement* rather than life-enhancing directions. This need for control is a mental obstacle to the freedom that the mind requires to concentrate naturally and productively— to gain *geniune* control through choice and inner discipline rather than through slavery to the *need* for it. The key to learning is within yourself, but you must overcome the mental blocks of self-imposed rules and criticism. Before you can master the college classroom, you must learn to master yourself. In other words, you must learn to trust your mind to learn without continuous conscious instruction and correction. You learn best when you put aside mental judgments of your performance, positive *or* negative.

Trust

Students are constantly thinking about how well they are doing. They rush around comparing grades, measuring themselves against one another, or even against themselves. Their minds are so busy with evaluation that they risk diminishing their actual performance. Competition and evaluation is a way to motivate yourself, but the motivational source is external, not internal. It is like being a horse that pulls a carriage only when it is offered a carrot or whipped. Inherent in this form of motivation is negative evaluation:

"You could have done better. You should have studied harder!"

"What makes you think you can learn French anyway?"

"You'll never be as good as your roommate!"

These voices originate with others; you learn them, and you can defeat yourself before you have even given yourself a real chance. Such self-criticism implies a secret fear that you are not as good as you want to be. Chances are, you are actually much more talented and able to learn than you believe.

Your mind possesses an innate sense of exploration. It *wants* to learn. Learning is part of survival. It also aims toward excellence, once it is free from the influence of debilitating criticism. The more you let go of external obsessions and evaluations, the more energy is freed for your inner resources to achieve. And with achievement comes increased motivation, increased pleasure, and better performance, not because you focused on it, but because you *allowed* it to happen.

We often see amazing feats performed by athletes. A running back may catch a football when it seemed not just unlikely that he could, but *impossible!* A tennis player will get to a ball and send it back over the net for a winner when we were sure she would never get near the ball. Often the athletes who perform these feats are as surprised and delighted as the spectators. They simply allowed their bodies to go, and their bodies performed beyond even their own high expectations. Tennis star Billie Jean King once expressed the feelings she had during such a performance: "...my concentration is so perfect it almost seems as though I'm able to transport myself beyond the turmoil of the court to some place of peace and calm. I know where the ball is on every shot, and it always looks as big and well-defined as a basketball. Just a huge thing I couldn't miss if I wanted to. I've got perfect control of the match, my rhythm and movements are excellent, everything in total balance." This feeling occurred not because she concentrated on rhythm, balance and control but because she had prepared herself to play, knew *how* to play and concentrated on just doing it. She trusted herself and the trust paid off in greater ways than she had dreamed.

But how can you let go and just trust your mind to learn what you need for the exam?

First, forget the exam. The important thing is to learn the subject. Your performance on the exam will take care of itself, because you will have learned holistically rather than piecemeal, and you will have a context in which the questions on the exam make sense.

When Janet first learned statistics, it seemed confusing and pointless to her but she memorized the formulas, one by one. The exams seemed hard, and even though she performed well enough to get a good grade, she felt that she had not really understood what statistics was about. So she set about to learn more, to set those formulas into a sensible context. She had only the motivation to learn the subject to keep her going. There would be no more exams. Yet, gradually, she learned enough to actually find errors in the text. When she looked back over the exams, they seemed exceedingly simple and she had a hard time believing they had once seemed so difficult. She could have done them in half the time she actually took had she learned the *subject* rather than just memorizing formulas, and done better, with less stress!

As with the water experiment, the more you focus on keeping track of the externals, like learning for the punishment/reward system offered by an exam, the less free is your inner mind to use the energy it needs to yield its best results.

Great ideas often occur to people who have decided to

trust their minds rather than to force answers to puzzling problems. They receive sudden, fully formed inspirations, seemingly from nowhere. The image is born spontaneously rather than painstakingly constructed out of data and techniques. For example, a computer analyst was working on diagrams for computer memory and information security. He drew one which was original and highly creative. He stared at it and saw that it was perfect for what he needed to do. Yet he insisted that the design had taken him by surprise. Many successful people echo similar experiences. Novelist Louis L'Amour once said that he loves to write because he cannot wait to see what his characters are going to say and do. The same thing can happen in an academic context.

A graduate student was assigned to do a lecture on a concept of Kant's which he did not understand. He went to books and tried very hard to make sense of it before the next day's class. He used all the tools of rational analysis that he knew, to no avail. Finally exhausted, he went to sleep, still unable to piece together a coherent lecture on the subject. Yet the next day, the lecture fell into place "like magic," and for the first time, he actually understood Kant's formulation.

So what does it mean to trust your mind to learn?

First of all, it may seem like a contradiction to talk about disciplining yourself to achieve spontaneity and enjoyment. However, both discipline and the sense of control that are essential to inner learning actually coordinate so well that you perform them *without* feeling the effort exerted to discipline yourself in some activity that you dislike. Just as work and play *seem* to be opposites, there is a way to develop your work to achieve the *qualities* of play. Discipline and control (not the need, but the exercise of choice) are simply part of the process that results in spontaneity and creativity.

Now, back to inner direction. Rather than attempting to spell out something that might then only become part of your parent-child cycle of conscious instruction, you will now get the chance to experience for yourself the feeling of allowing your mind to work as an inner skill that engages the energy of your body.

_____ Practicing Trust

Clasp your hands in front of you. Notice which thumb is on top. Now unclasp then reclasp them to get the other thumb on top. It will probably take a conscious effort to break your physical habit, and the action will feel uncomfortable. Yet you can do it. That is, you can perform *differently* from the way you are used to, and in doing so, see that the fact that one thumb usually ends up on top is not necessarily the "right" way to do it. It is just the way you are *used* to doing it. You can develop the same sort of reorganizing in your mental life to achieve the flexibility needed to trust your inner resources, even if it seems uncomfortable at first.

There is much that we do automatically. We get into certain mental habits that track our minds a certain way. It gives us stability, predictability, structure, and efficiency. We are taught a certain approach to a problem, we learn it, then generalize that same approach to other problems. It works, so we continue to use that approach, to the point where we believe it to be the "only" one or the "best" one. However, learning implies change of some sort. Habitual patterns can become a hindrance.

Try this problem. Subtract 178 from 365. Pay attention to the method you use and describe how you did it.

Now sit back and think about how you might have achieved the same result with a different process. It may take you some time to come up with an alternative. You may not be able to do it at all, but try. There *is* another way. Do not go on to the next paragraph until you have given this exercise a shot. (You want to learn how to trust your mind, don't you?) Don't force it. Relax and allow yourself to *see* it.

There are two approaches to subtraction methods typically taught in elementary school. You will have learned one or the other. Whichever one is new to you might surprise you. But set up a few subtraction problems and try it.

1. Subtract the lower number in the right hand column from the upper number in that column. If the lower number is larger, add ten to the upper number, borrowed from the digit to the left (which may, in turn have to borrow ten from the digit to *its* left). Then write the difference at the rightmost digit of the answer. Move one column to the left. If ten was added in the preceding step, decrease the top number by one. Continue the process until you have found the entire numerical difference between the top and bottom numbers.

2. Subtract the lower number in the right hand column from the upper number. If the lower is larger, add ten to the upper number and subtract. Write the difference as the right hand digit. Move one column to the left. If ten was added in the preceding step, increase the lower number by one. If the lower is larger, add ten to the upper number, then subtract. Repeat this step until the problem is solved.

The two approaches get the same result, but your habit of using one probably prevented you from seeing the possibility of the other. Do a few more problems with the method that is new to you to get a feel for breaking out of your habit. You'll see that they are equally effective. You may believe one is faster than the other, but that is only because you have practiced it more.

This mental habituation can have larger scale consequences in the classroom. An ethics professor once attempted to involve her students in a unique discussion format in her Medical Ethics course. She set up panel discussions in a talk-show format. The students were confused. They had been trained to think of the "correct" classroom manner of holding discussions as a response to a lecture, or as a debate. She went ahead with her plan but the students just would not cooperate. What could have been a unique, interesting, and enjoyable course was bogged down in rigid mental habits. What I pointed out earlier as a fear of responsibility and change has another side: the students were unable to trust themselves to learn in any way but the one they were used to.

As an exercise in trust, try the following riddles. You may have seen some before, so skip them and move on to the ones you don't know. Don't give up when you feel frustrated. Instead, relax and allow the answer to come to you. You may have more success if you don't try too hard to figure them out. The answers are at the end of Part 2, p. 192, but don't peek until you have really given yourself a chance.

1. Two American coins equal thirty cents, but one of them is not a nickel. What are the two coins?

2. You are standing on a marble floor. How can you drop a raw egg five feet without breaking its shell?

3. You go to bed at eight o'clock and set the alarm for nine. How many hours of sleep will you get?

4. A cabdriver picked up a woman who gave her address, then talked nonstop. He motioned to her that he was deaf so she remained quiet the rest of the trip. When she was dropped off and had paid her fare, she realized he had lied to her. How?

5. The patient was the son of the surgeon, yet the surgeon was not the boy's father. Explain this.

6. One month has twenty-eight days. Of the remaining eleven, how many have thirty days?

7. Why can't a man living in New York be buried west of the Mississippi?

8. Do they have a fourth of July in England?

9. How many times can you subtract the numeral two from the numeral twenty-four?

10. A car trip of one hundred miles took two hours, yet no one noticed that one tire was flat. How was this possible?

Chances are, if you figured out the answers (without having heard them before,) you had to stumble through mental habits which either hindered a quick answer or led you to wrong answers. For example, the question about the fourth of July in England seems obvious, yet we associate the fourth of July so strongly with our independence day, that we say England has no fourth of July. Of course they do! They just do not celebrate it like we do. For them, it is merely the day after the third of July.

Part of learning to trust your mind is learning to relax mental habits. Easier said than done, of course, but still a necessity. We tend to want to cling to what we are used to, yet an approach that works in one context might cripple us in another. For example, if you believe you can only learn in a solitary manner, you will be unable to adapt yourself to the learning opportunities of discussions or group work. Or if you believe that the only way to learn how to write a paper is to use an instructional text, you will feel insecure with a professor who teaches without such a text.

Trust is an essential ingredient in mental agility—of *trying out* something new. The trick is not to trust a single approach but to trust your mind to *adapt,* and to see its way through a problem to a solution, even if the method of getting there seems uncomfortable or strange. It is only uncomfortable because you have not been taught it, not because it does not work.

If you rely on old mental habits, and they fail to get you what you want, the result is that you will increase your effort to make those "tried-and-true" habits work. Trying too hard cuts off the energy flow of your mind. It makes you tense and often frustrates you. Frustration reinforces the block. Sometimes a new approach will get you what you want very quickly.

Clinging to mental habits can also make you prone to self-judgment. Self-judgment can hinder performance. When you are "on the spot," you tend to stiffen, and try to be too careful about doing things just right. The free flow which can put a creative edge on your activity is missing. It is like trying to paint a picture or write a poem according to what *someone else* dictates. Your movement is constricted, your concentration divided, your results stiff. Given the freedom to just allow your inner self to paint without judgment can often surprise you with the fluidity and perfection that you attempted to achieve for "the judge," but which too much care to do it "right" hindered you from achieving.

When I began this chapter, I set a goal of completing a certain number of pages. I wanted so much to reach that goal, that I started to force the ideas. I ended up with one-third the number of pages I wanted, no inspiration, and I did not enjoy what I wrote. So I let my mind take over.

Suddenly I found that I met my quota and had even gone beyond. The writing was fluid and fun, even exciting. My initial frustration and effort had blocked me, but when I allowed my mind the freedom of expression, the chapter unfolded into directions neither planned nor forced, but which were better than what I *had* previously planned.

If you have ever experienced something like this, take a moment to recall the details and the feelings.

Your mind can be an automatic doer if you allow it. And that is the key: *allowing* rather than forcing. Allow your mind to learn, to recall, to perform. *Trust* yourself. Set simple precise goals, and then put aside your judgmental, instructing self. *Do* what you want to do.

Clearly, this does not mean that you can sit back and say, "okay, mind, do it all for me." You will need to prepare yourself. That is, if you want fluid recall, you have to read the text. If you want performance, you will need to know the material. If you want to learn, you will need to motivate yourself to be ready. "Allowing" simply means to go ahead and do something that you *can* do—allowing the inner self to get into gear—rather than losing time and depleting energy by *telling* yourself how to do it right.

This approach will seem risky to you. You already know how to get a good grade and you are afraid to let go of old habits, constricting as they may be. This is what trust is about. Confronting the risk. Going ahead despite fear and insecurity. Having courage and using it to gird your confidence with the possibility that you will come out ahead.

We associate the unfamiliar with being painful or frightening. We see potential loss more easily than potential gain. Such associations block us from experiencing something that can be more exciting and creative than approaches we take now. Take that bold step to try something new and *believe* that your risk will pay off in something greater than does your current approach. It has worked for countless people, from artists to athletes to business executives. There is no reason why it cannot work for you.

You can strengthen your resolve to trust your mind by affirming that it can, indeed, take you where you want to go. The first steps are the hardest. You may need conscious self-affirmation the most when you first let go. When success occurs, acknowledge it and use it as further motivation until you achieve an inner sense of confidence. Soon, letting go, trusting, and affirming will become natural mental habits.

You may find yourself not just learning a computer language to get by in a class, but actually *inventing* one. You may be able not only to "figure out" answers, but also to come up with creative new problems, or a more efficient method for solving old problems (or spot errors made by the author of your text). There is much that can come out of an active, alert, motivated mind that is not impeded by restrictions. Certainly more will be gained, at the very least, in allowing your mind to perform to its energy potential, than in simply reducing it to a mechanical tool to get you through a course. Coupled with visualization for increased mental power, there is no telling how far you can go!

_____ Summary

We waste time and energy when we insist on conscious self instruction and criticism. Direction should come from within as affirmation from the unconscious mind—the automatic doer, where performance is not hindered by judgment or piecemeal steps. The inner mind can perceive and perform holistically, often yielding fully structured images that accurately target solutions to problems. By trusting our mind/body coordination the way athletes do, we may learn and perform well beyond our own expectations, with more fluidity and enjoyment than conscious self-criticism (or even rule-oriented praise) allow.

Exercise ———————————————————————

1. Draw five rows of trees with four in each row to get only ten trees.

2. Use only four straight lines to connect all the dots.

(Solutions on p. 192)

11

Being Still

Too much hurry, too much worry characterizes the mood of our culture. There is so much to do and not enough time in which to do it. Who has time for sitting still?

The techniques of inner direction and visualization rely on relaxation and on cultivating a certain stillness of mind. The same applies to the skill of concentration, which depends heavily on your ability to achieve a focused, uncluttered mind.

We marvel at the concentration level of athletes and artists. That they can sustain such intense focus for long periods seems beyond the abilities of most of us, although we may hunger for the rewards—amazing stamina and extraordinary performance. The art of inner learning can put you in touch with those powers by revealing to you your own levels of concentration and your ability to experience the state of "flow." Flow is the experience of "peak performers" who attain the greatest degree of quality and creativity in what they do.

Receptivity

The focused mind must be a receptive mind. This is not a state of passivity that merely absorbs. It is an open, relaxed *alertness*. Clear reception results from minimizing interferences. Self-instruction and self-criticism are just two potential sources for interference. Each day we encounter situations that demand our attention. In college, those situations can be quite complicated, bombarding us with a continuous tug of war in all directions:

"I've got an exam in statistics today and a paper for composition due on Thursday. I've also got to read thirty pages for psychology for tomorrow and meet with my study group. But my parents want me home for the weekend. So I'll have to work extra hours in the cafeteria on Friday in order to get away. But Sandy wants to go out on Friday to see this great new movie. And I haven't yet done my laundry!"

It is difficult to put psychological brackets around all of this "noise" and ready the mind to be still. Yet the kind of learning targeted by this book rests on a foundation of concentration, the basis of which is a still, receptive mind.

Think about some of the exercises you did in the chapter on inner direction. Getting the answers was less a matter of intense calculation than of sudden insight into the structure of the problem. To get that insight, you had to have a receptive mind—an inner ability to allow the structure to show itself to you so that you can find a means of resolving it. But there is more to it than just perception and intelligence. You must also be ready to recognize solutions from *wherever* they come.

You would hardly be ready if you were thinking about too many other things.

Annie Dillard, in her book *Pilgrim at Tinker Creek,* portrays this attitude of quiet, uncluttered receptivity. She walks through the woods for long stretches of time, not actively looking for events to happen, but simply relaxes her mind enough to be ready for noticing. If she were *looking* for a woodpecker, let's say, she might be so concerned to find one that she could miss the beautiful goldfinch. Or if she were thinking about other things she had to do that day, she might miss a woodpecker right in front of her. Instead of narrowing her vision too much, or cluttering it, she has learned to focus in an open state of readiness. She allows nature spontaneously to appear to her as it is, rather than deciding what she wants to see. As a result, she witnesses remarkable natural phenomena that a busier mind would miss.

Were Annie Dillard to bring this presence of mind, this

stillness, to the classroom, no doubt she would hear many things in a lecture or discussion that passes over the heads of students who are distracted with the multiple directions of their lives.

A group of students were asked to do an exercise from a hospice for a class on Philosophies of Death and Dying, that required that they find a place alone and sit for ten minutes, thinking about what death means to them. They were to close their eyes, lie on the floor in the dark, and imagine what it would be like to be dead.

When this exercise was assigned, there were nervous titters over the strange nature of the assignment. Not everyone did it. A number of students felt that they could figure out what it was like without actually doing the exercise— just a matter of a few moments of imagination. However, those who actually did the exercise found, to their surprise, that thinking about it and doing it were worlds apart. Many of them discovered things about themselves, alone in the dark, that they had never realized:

"I was really afraid of death. I wouldn't have admitted to that if I hadn't done this exercise."

"I was scared at first, but then I found a sense of peace that I had never anticipated."

"I understood for the first time what it must have been like for my mother to lose my father."

In the stillness of this exercise, and in the open-ended structure, the students relaxed into a receptive state where images come freely and insight is born. They did not know what to expect so they did not verbally instruct their minds, and were thus free to "listen" to their inner self-expression. This is the ideal state of mind for poets and artists, writers and mathematicians, and for the birth of any sort of creative endeavor. The Romantic poets actively sought stillness as the place where they came closest to ultimate inspiration.

This form of stillness may seem to contradict the notion that setting goals is important to learning, but that is not the case. You can set goals and still free your mind to be alert to ways of getting there that you do not readily perceive when you think through the steps in ordinary ways. It is the same idea as using control to achieve spontaneity. It is not a contradiction but the joining of two seemingly opposed concepts to create a state of mind and experience that utilizes both. Without goals, a receptive mind is aimless. With goals, it has direction but is not blocked by that direction. You set goals, but you do not become obsessed with them. You can relax and still get to them, like setting opposite banks to water for the free flow of a river.

To become receptive, you must slow your mind to free it of distractions that produce mental noise. Try to be aware of only the present, not the future or the past. Use your powers of visualization for this. Simply concentrate on being where you are right now. What are you doing? Is your foot tapping, your jaw tense? Be aware of yourself. How do different parts of your body *feel?* Do you hear anything? Smell anything? What does your tongue feel like? Your hands? Relax. Do not worry about wasting time or having something else to do. Harness the natural energy within and make it still.

It is not a matter of telling yourself to be still, but of simply *being still*—allowing that sense of inner direction to take over.

Being receptive is also not the result of actively suppressing your worries and concerns, because to do so makes you focus on them, and also allows them to become stressful in other ways. That only makes you more tense. Simply let them go for the moment. Practice letting them go for longer and longer periods. Then apply this skill to practical situations.

For example, if you are in the middle of a class and suddenly remember that you forgot to lock your car door, or that you have a paper due in two days for another class, use the opportunity to learn to let the problem go. It will only hinder you in learning to be receptive if you focus on these worries. You can do nothing about them, anyway, until you leave that class. Refocus your mind. Be still. Such situations provide the best practical opportunities to sharpen this skill.

Becoming still progresses through two stages. First, there

is physical relaxation. Then, as the body relaxes, the mind can grow more patient and attentive. You are ready, without being tense, for the instantaneous action you might need to respond to that which is evident only if you are alert and open to it.

You can use the technique of visualization to achieve stillness. Concentrate first on your body, part by part, in a comfortable position. Then clear your mind of pressures and distractions. Imagine yourself in a peaceful place, like on an empty beach. With enough practice, you can allow your inner instruction to take over, ensuring stillness whenever you need it.

Your learning potential lies dormant within stillness, but the stillness can be unnerving. You feel vulnerable, naked. You are encountering your most intimate self, not sure what you will find. It can be frightening, but it can also be rewarding.

_____ The Rewards

Having a still, receptive mind allows you to stay with the subject being taught. Your mind should connect with the subject, and will only do so if it is free of unnecessary distractions. It is similar to the way children learn about the world. They are curious and intense, unencumbered by biases and worries, and simply take it all in. They see more than we do and they have more fun with what they see. Go for a walk with a child if you have a chance. Listen to what he or she says. You will see familiar sights in new ways, and perhaps get a sense of the sort of alert receptivity that makes such perspectives possible.

You may believe that a quiet, awed simplicity is no longer available to you, because you have responsibilities and concerns. You are no longer a child. However, there is no reason why you cannot be both responsible and receptive. The art of inner learning adopts the childlike openness that energizes the alert mind. It is accessible to anyone who wants to develop and practice it.

Athletes learn this sort of stillness and receptivity. Even in the midst of cheering fans, professional athletes can block out the distractions and allow the mental flow of energy that assists them in focusing on the situation as it changes from one moment to the next. If tennis players, for example, allow themselves to think about the shot they missed, or about the one they hope to hit, they take their focus off hitting the one coming that moment.

The same thing happens in the classroom when you allow yourself to become distracted. You take the focus off your learning—you *miss* things—and gain nothing to help get your car locked or your paper done for another class. You lose what was available to you *right then,* in *that* class.

There is power in the deeply hidden self, a wealth of spontaneous creativity waiting to be tapped. While the journey within may seem dark, mysterious, and perhaps a bit intimidating, it is an avenue toward mental clarity and definition. Silence of this sort is too often alien. We associate it with loneliness and vulnerability instead of with self-strengthening solitude. Silence is used in movies as the moment preceding the ultimate horrors. We are too afraid of silence. However, as with risk and confusion, there is a positive side, and that side must be acknowledged if you are to develop the art of inner learning.

Still waters run the deepest. If we remain at the surface, our learning will be superficial, our concentration fleeting, and the results mediocre, even for students who excel within the traditional system. Only with a quiet mind will you achieve the deepest levels of concentration.

Like Annie Dillard, we can reap the benefits of a world teeming with secret activities only if we develop patience, only if we unburden ourselves of the need to worry and to hurry, and only if we pause for a few moments to understand and practice the value of the still and receptive mind.

_____ Self-Awareness vs. Self-Consciousness

It may seem as if, to this point, you have been taught so much that it is impossible to develop stillness. There is simply too much to remember, to think about, to practice! Again, the *initial* period of developing a skill will involve confusion as you attempt to keep track of everything you must do. However, as you get used to it, much will fall into place automatically and the development of an inner stillness becomes possible. As you learn to concentrate and use imagery, and as you feel the experience of absorbed, energetic concentration, you will see how it all comes together without worry or force on your part. Perhaps the most distracting element will be the idea of maintaining your self-awarenss.

While it is important to be aware of your style of learning, noting your strengths and weaknesses, in order to facilitate a more effective involvement in your education, you can become so overly concerned with your self-examination that you become self-conscious. It is one thing to take note of your style through double reflection. It is quite another to become analytic, critical, or proud of it.

When we become self-conscious, we put our "selves" too much in the foreground for effective learning to take place. We typically either think too highly of ourselves or too little of ourselves. Stillness can be part of self-examination, but not of self-consciousness. The point of self-awareness is to become aware in order gradually to move away from what blocks you, not to get wrapped up in yourself.

In the next chapter, the focus is on deep concentration, which can be achieved only when the mind has been stilled.

Summary

The still mind will bring you nearer to the art of inner learning by clearing away the background noise of everyday concerns. You can use imagery to help to achieve it, but it must become one of your skills if you are to experience the level of concentration and sense of centeredness that is essential to establishing an involved inter-relationship with the subject you are learning. Such a relationship is characteristic of true education.

Since stillness is part of the overall exercise of concentration, there are no separate exercises suggested; however, you may choose to use visualization to practice relaxation before moving on to concentration.

12

Concentration

In *The Method of Zen,* Eugen Herrigel describes a time when he was in Japan for a meeting on the fifth floor of a hotel. Suddenly there was a low rumble. The building swayed and objects began to crash to the floor. Everyone was alarmed, recalling a terrible earthquake a few years earlier, and most of the people present rushed out into the halls. Herrigel was about to run when he noticed one of his Japanese colleagues had not moved. Instead, the man sat in the midst of the chaos, completely calm, hands folded, his eyes closed as if he were unconcerned about the potential danger. Spellbound, Herrigel watched him. The earthquake lasted a long time, and when it was over, the Japanese man continued the conversation at precisely the point where it had broken off. The man had put himself into a state of "unassailable" concentration.

So far you have learned about inner direction, trust, and stillness as prerequisites for achieving the most effective type of concentration for learning. You are about to be invited into the inner circle of focused concentration. Imagine yourself sitting as calmly as the Japanese businessman, while you take an exam or listen to a complex lecture. It *is* possible, but first you must learn about the levels of awareness.

In this chapter, I will cover three levels of awareness and discuss how they affect your classroom performance. The next chapter is a discussion of the experience of sustaining the deepest level—the most absorbed form of concentration, akin to that of Herrigel's Japanese colleague.

_____ First Level

Most of your everyday encounters involve a sort of diffuse, scanning awareness. You possess a half-conscious sense of where you are and what you are doing, but you are not paying close attention to any of it. As I discussed in the chapter on double reflection, there is much more sensory stimulation going on at any given moment than you *can* be aware of, and this stimulation becomes a part of your experience without intruding much on your attention. Your body is breathing, your tongue is moist, you are walking past a blur of buildings and you are only vaguely aware of any of it. Your body takes over in an automatic fashion, allowing you to walk or drive or breathe without having to take any particular notice of your surroundings. Often this "automatic pilot" occurs before you have paid close enough attention to really know what you are doing. Much of the substance of your day-to-day encounters is simply absorbed into the unnoticed, marginal consciousness that gives context to your life.

This sort of awareness provides the foundation from which you move into other levels of awareness and concentration. To get a better sense of what I mean, look at some item in the room in which you are now sitting, for example, a chair. You can see the chair because there is a background wall against which your eyes can focus on the chair. The chair stands as a figure against the background. If you refocus your eyes to take more notice of the background (the wall), you will lose a defined perception of the chair.

We cannot perceive everything with the same degree of awareness. Some of what we perceive recedes so as to allow a more defined perception of other things. We need background in order to see figures. Likewise, we need this ordinary, everyday unfocused level of awareness to make our world congeal in a way that makes sense to us. It is at the second level of awareness that we begin to form more distinct impressions.

_____ Second Level

Only when you want to, or are startled into becoming more aware do you take enough interest in your body, thoughts, or environment to begin to attend more specifically to something that grabs your attention. You stumble on a cracked sidewalk and you suddenly notice the sidewalk, or your injured toe. You arrive at your destination and you notice the building or room, perhaps even your body's nervousness if you happen to be going to the dentist. Your tooth hurts, so you notice an area of your body that otherwise remains unobtrusive. When you notice, you isolate the figure from its background. Something stands out to you, like seeing a person you know in a crowd. It is this more *defined* awareness that draws you into the second level.

What turns one thing into "figure" rather than another is its significance to you. You wrap it in some kind of emotional coating, like discomfort, delight, or interest. Otherwise, it is just something that exists for you as part of a context. For example, a friend might mention a certain building on campus, believing you *must* know where it is because you pass it everyday. Yet, because you've never really taken note of it, you can rightly claim ignorance. In one sense, you've seen it, physically, but not in a way that impressed your memory. Nothing about the building caused you to set it apart from any other.

Now suppose you have a class in this building. Suddenly it becomes significant to you in the context of your needs and interests. You discover its name, its location, and how to get to it. The building has become a focal point in your otherwise passive scanning. Your mind has quickened to it.

However, this type of awareness is often quickly absorbed into your passive mental modes. Your mind forms a memorable impression of the building, based on its meaning for you, yet the "figure" formed at this level of awareness can easily be pushed into a background, where you automatically "know" where you are going, and you do get to the building you want, but your awareness diminishes into a simple stimulus-response scenario requiring little or no conscious reflection over what you are doing.

To make this more meaningful to you, before going on with the text, think of something from your own life that illustrates the distinction between these levels of awareness, where something from the background stood out to you, then eventually became just another aspect of the background.

The second level of reflection involves varying degrees of attention, from passive to active to full consciousness. Although you are more fully engaged with the world in this level than in the first level, you may derive little more than a short-term benefit from it, especially as the experience, event, or object of significance fades from your awareness. This can be a step toward inner direction, but getting to this point and no further offers only routine avenues to superficial knowledge. What does this process have to do with you as a student?

After the initial period of getting yourself oriented in the classroom, this "interested awareness" fades to the level of awareness that becomes more passive than attentive. Many students attend class out of habit or fear of reprisal; they sit in a seat and spread out their notebooks; they pick up their pens. It's all automatic. Then, as the lecture unfolds, they take notes. Automatic. Often they are not thinking about what is being taught to them, but simply taking notes because that is their function as students.

While they are no longer just scanning at the first level of awareness, their attention is only minimally focused on what they are doing. The words of the lecture stand out as "figure" from background only insofar as they might appear on an exam or might be significant in some other assignment. Students dutifully take them down, but have turned off their minds to opportunities for active comprehension. This level of awareness is a common practice, but it is altogether inadequate as a tool for learning, especially in its least attentive form.

The problem, however, is that many students simply do not know about deeper forms of concentration, or if they do, they perceive those forms as something over which they have little control or as requiring too much effort. However, the third level of awareness is not as far from the reach of most students as they think, and this level will deliver more educational benefits as well as more enjoyment in the classroom than do the first two.

_____ Third Level

Georgeann was frustrated to discover that her note-taking was interfering with her concentration on the lecture of a course she was taking. While she was writing, she was no longer listening, and as a consequence, her notes represented only chunks of the lecture. Finally, she stopped trying to take down the lecture verbatim and began to really listen. She made brief notes only when she felt an important idea needed further attention from her, or when she wanted to anchor the discussion at some significant point. She started to ask questions, then began to initiate discussion directions. Soon she was reading material outside the class. Georgeann was practicing the third level of awareness—the active, engaged mind. This is the point at which the art of inner learning really begins.

Before going on to read about this form of awareness, use your own experience to give it some context. Think about the differences in quality of attention between learning about a subject that you find interesting and attending a course that you find boring. You may want to exercise some imagery here to make those differences vivid.

The third level frequently occurs when you are genuinely interested in a subject, and not just attending class because "you have to be there to pass the course." At this level, you are absorbed in what you are learning, and you find the subject exciting and stimulating. The subject matter seems clear to you because you are following it, step by step, and your mind is anticipating, desiring more. Ironically, although this level requires more mental energy, comprehension is much more fluid. The subject is easier to grasp and retain, making the effort seem more like working toward a desired goal than like unrewarding drudgery.

This is the level of awareness that enables athletes to see the seams on the ball as it approaches them, or gives artists a sudden, holistic sense of structure. Everything seems slower, more relaxed, because your *mind* has picked up *its* pace. Relative to your mind's active participation, the lecture *is* slower. Your mind is no longer burdened by the lethargic attention of the passive form of the second level of awareness, which soon tires you out. Instead, your mind has become alert and involved. You study the subject of your major with this sort of attention, because (it may be assumed) this is the subject you have chosen and want to learn. Energy breeds energy, and breeds it best in this state of *relaxed* alertness.

At this level, you begin to forget yourself. You are not as concerned with the externals of grades, exams, comparisons. You are concerned about the *subject*. To learn it is a goal worthy in itself and thus had no *necessary* connection with a means-to-end success or an ego-booster. You are relaxed, less tense, more aware of the subject itself. Small distractions, such as classroom overcrowding, pipes knocking overhead, or lack of air-conditioning no longer divert you as they would if you were less involved and passive. Your mind grows still, uncluttered, and focused on the present. You are aware of what you are hearing now. Your mind does not invent distractions to keep itself busy because it is gathered toward a central focus. You are no longer *trying* to learn, but are actually *learning*. The need to control the process had dropped away and *inner* direction takes over. Altough the mind is in fast gear, it is calm—unassailable!

_____ Comparison

You can see how these levels of awareness differ when you think about the different ways that you read for a course. Select a subject that you have recently studied and recall as much as possible some specific details of that experience, and see how you fare in comparison with the description below.

On the first level, you scan the assignment, but your mind is not really on what you are doing. You find that you can read whole paragraphs without remembering a single word that came before your eyes. You read it over again, but still fail to retain very much of the material. This is because you are reading mechanically, allowing your eyes to move as they ought to move when they "read," yet your mind is disengaged from the task. You have divided mind from body, and the material is lost somewhere in between.

In a similar way, if you go to class with this sort of passive, disengaged awareness, you waste your time. Your body sits in the seat, your hand holds a pencil, you set the notebook in front of you, and maybe you even capture a few items to list on the paper, but your mind is not really involved or coordinated with the mechanics of your body. The division of energy tires you out and actually hinders your learning. You find that it takes much more than the physical mechanics of sitting at a desk taking notes or of scanning words in a textbook to learn anything.

At the second level, you are focused enough to comprehend the words on the page, and you retain a little bit, possibly even enough to pass an exam, but you typically forget most of what you read within a short period of time. The second level does not sustain itself for long, especially as other things, like a sports event or the pressure of other assignments, arise to distract your attention. While you are more alert at this level, it is still a more passive than active approach; as though your mind were an imprinting machine, which is cleared once there is no longer a need for the data. In the classroom, this level of awareness is not the complete waste of time that the first level of awareness is, but your gains are typically short-term and fragmented. You probably could not carry on an extensive, intelligent conversation about the subject. If you approach your college *major* with this level of awareness, and then hope to reap benefits for your career, you will be in for a rude surprise!

The passive attention that becomes inevitable at the second level does little to help you to retain and apply what you read or hear.

The third level *involves* you. When you read, you get a comprehensive picture, a context into which to fit each paragraph. When you confront something that seems out of place or nonsensical, you recognize it right away and you have some background with which to try to figure out why you are confused or stymied. You feel the flow of the material and experience a satisfied sense of closure when you finish reading. You tend to retain the material longer because you learned *the material,* not just "the items for an exam." You are more relaxed because you allow yourself to learn, rather than forcing the information in a stress-ridden attempt to fulfill external conditions.

In the classroom, this sort of awareness will serve you in the same way. You are ready to ask questions about concepts that confuse you, and challenge those with which you can intelligently disagree. You have developed a keen awareness of the subject that transcends your own ego hunger (e.g., the need to show off, the need to control, the need to be perfect). You are not "thinking yourself into" learning, but, instead, you are really absorbed by something that grows even more interesting and stimulating as you learn about it.

The rewards of learning at this third level are inherent in your manner of involvement. At the first level, there are few rewards because the mind is too unfocused. There is no defined figure to background. At the second level, the rewards are typically external (a passing mark on a paper or an exam) and short-lived. At this third level, however, you are finding out things of interest to you, broadening your understanding, feeling more confident of your grasp of the material, getting more involved in the course, and laying a foundation for a respectable and knowledgeable position on detailed aspects of the subject. You can argue about things, such as the merits of quantum physics over the Newtonian model, because you have confidence in what you are saying. Your excitement over learning leads you to find out more, which in turn, yields even greater rewards. You can more readily perceive ways to apply what you have learned, rather than just letting it sit "in your head," or in your college notebooks. You become more like the skilled, caring craftsman than the bored assembly-line worker.

It is likely that you have experienced this third level of awareness to some degree during your education. You may understand what I mean when I talk about being absorbed and enjoying what you learn. It feels like the sort of involvement that you experience with a hobby or a sport. However, I would not be surprised if your impression of this state is that it "just comes upon you," and that you have no real control over it. This is, however, a misunderstanding of your own mind. I have talked about discipline and practice. Those are exactly the ingredients you need, along with stillness, to consistently achieve this third level of awareness. Once again, imagery can assist you to gain control over how you participate in your education. If you practice envisioning yourself relaxed and alert in the classroom, you will become what you envision.

To maximize a capacity for third level awareness, you will need to master the fundamentals covered in preceding chapters: preparation, physical health, ego freedom, an uncluttered mind, an ability to "let go" of a controlling or critical attitude, and a sense of inner discipline through which you can break the bad habits of poorly focused thinking. Like holding your breath, you can increase your capacity with practice.

For example, a good exercise is to focus on some simple objects in your environment—a pencil or a paper clip—for five minutes. Your mind will no doubt wander. Count how many times in the five-minute period it wanders. Then do the exercise again and keep track. Keep repeating it until you have managed to cut down on the amount of times you lose concentration. It *is* under your control, more than you might realize. You can apply this kind of exercise in the classroom as well.

The third level of awareness is where deep concentration

and true learning begin, but only if you develop two skills in order to reach and stay at this level: 1) listening, and 2) finding your personal "groove."

Listening

We live in a culture where the media is very powerful, and where people are more comfortable with noise than with silence. Inevitably, a lot of people talk without having much to say (including college professors). There is only so much you can listen to before you lose the edge on your alertness.

The art of listening is a lot more difficult than many people believe. It involves more than just *hearing*. Because it is an element of self-awareness, the process of developing listening skills also involves three levels of awareness. Merely hearing sounds, for example, is like the unfocused background awareness of the first level. Passive listening and taking temporary note of certain sounds is the second level, while listening with an involved alertness draws on and strengthens the sort of concentration offered at the third level.

Think about your own style of listening. You've probably experienced all three levels. Where you live, you are so used to the typical noises there that you pay no real attention to them, but if a new sound intruded—especially if it signaled danger, like a fire alarm—you would take note. You have probably experienced the form of listening common among many students, of hearing with "half an ear" to a lecture that does not stimulate you but to which you must be attentive in order to pass the course. You may also have had some experience with the alert form of listening that involves you fully. Use visualization to become more aware of the differences and the tendencies of your own style of listening.

Anyone can hear, if their physical organs are functioning properly. But not everyone knows how to listen. Sometimes we attend to what someone else is saying with an agenda intact. We are thinking about what we are going to say, or about what we heard someone else say on the subject, or about why we do or do not agree with what the speaker is saying. Our minds are so full of self-centered noises that we listen selectively, and may even completely retranslate what is said in order to make it comprehensible within our own belief systems. Students will sometimes tell me that I said something in a lecture or about an assignment that I know I would never have said, because the students are listening with an agenda through which they have filtered and distorted my actual words. The best way to listen is to attend to the present, hearing what is said *as* it is said, without worrying about whether you agree or disagree at the moment you hear it, and without trying to form a response or anticipate what will be said.

You may think that such undifferentiated listening would be ineffective—too much like passive listening. Yet in fact true listening retains a focus that is relaxed and attentive, not selective; it crystalizes the subject efficiently and effectively. You hear what is actually said, rather than what you are anticipating, or what you might want to hear; you attend to the speaker rather than to yourself; you experience the subject matter directly rather than filtered through your own concerns; you are alert, rather than hampered by too much mental activity; and you develop an awareness of what the subject *is* rather than what you *think* it is. The way you listen is like the way Annie Dillard walked around observing the world around her.

Think about listening as a skill similar to playing a video game. You cannot just decide what will happen, although you may have goals about what you would *like* to have happen; you have to follow the action of the game as it occurs, and typically at a very rapid pace. You need to stay calm, not tense, and to keep your mind alert and focused. You attend only to what you need to attend to, and your mind shuts out the distractions. People may be cheering you on, but you don't hear them. You are becoming one with the levers of the machine. This is analogous to developing good listening skills, which can be strengthened by deepening your ability to go past typical, everyday forms of awareness, and towards real concentration.

Finding Your Personal Groove

You have a lot of mental energy, and you can use this energy either positively or negatively. You can enhance your learning or hinder it. Energy translates into mental stimulation or into tension. It is your own habit of discipline that will decide whether your mental energy is going to be effective for you.

One way to set yourself into a positive direction is to view your attention to a subject as a relationship. You must be eager to pursue the relationship, and put sufficient time and energy into it if you are to derive any reward from it. Once you initiate a motivating attitude, the rewards will often roll in quickly. But first you must establish a "groove" or a set of habits that will keep you active, prepared, and motivated in the relationship. For example, when you are involved in a friendship, you make a point to call or talk to the friend on a fairly regular schedule. At first this takes effort. Then it becomes something you look forward to as you grow more acquainted. Similarly with learning; once you initiate the relationship and establish consistent habits of staying focused, alert, and interested, you will soon be ready for the experience that comes with the final stage of awareness.

Summary

The three levels of awareness move through a continuum from unfocused, to focused-but-passive, to focus-with-disciplined-alertness. Students often get stuck on a passive level, and as a consequence, the results and rewards of their classroom performance are typically mediocre. They are easily bored and distracted. The third level of awareness is a jump into the consistently active and alert frame of mind, opening a valve of mental energy. This energy needs disciplined channeling in order to turn it into stimulation rather than into tension. Once you have found this personal "groove" energy, the stage is set for the experience of absorbed, attentive focus, called "flow."

Excercises

1. If you did not do the exercise with the paper clip, do it now. Then think up three different ways you can apply to the classroom your new ability to concentrate.

2. Assess how deeply you tend to focus in the classroom. If you feel you need improvement, think of ways to do that. For example, if you are easily distracted by the noise of a heater, move to a different part of the room.

3. Do the same thing with the way you concentrate on reading a text.

*"We are what we repeatedly do.
Excellence, then, is not an act but
a habit."*

—Aristotle

13

Flow

J erry is working on a paper. He has gathered all the
research he needs, and has organized his notes. There is
nothing else that needs to be done before he sits down to
write. He clears his mind and begins to concentrate. Soon
he is immersed in his task. The ideas flow as freely as
water from an open faucet. Gradually, he grows unaware of
the sound of the heater, of the smell of pizza from next
door, of his own empty stomach. He does not know that
his fingers are cold or that he is thirsty. He is fully absorbed
in his project. Hours pass and he has no sense of time.
When he finally emerges, he is somewhat numb and hungry;
he also feels exhilarated and is suprised to find out how
much time has passed.

This is the experience of "flow." It is what athletes call
"getting into the groove," "playing out of my head," or
being "pumped up," "honed in," and "wired." Others have
named it the "Optimum Performance State," "Peak Performance State," and the "White Moment." It is the experience
of many professionals who enjoy their work, and the context
for excellence and quality in performance, when creativity
and energy run high, and external distractions are minimized to the point of perceptual nonexistence. It is also the
essence of the internal motivating force involved in the art
of inner learning.

Most people have experienced flow in one form or
another by the time they get to college. You understand
what it means to be so absorbed in something you are
doing that you fail to notice external distractions. Having
experienced it from time-to-time, you no doubt understand
how exhilarating it can be. For some people, it is almost

mystical. Yet you may be surprised to learn that flow is not necessarily just a pleasant experience that happens to you from time-to-time. Flow is something you can cultivate. Although it may seem sporadic and unpredictable, recent research has shown that you can improve your chances for making this productive and pleasurable state of consciousness part of your learning routine.

_____ Flow: The Context

The concept of flow has been closely associated with Japanese practices of Zen. "If one really wishes to master an art," says D. T. Suzuki, author of *Zen and Japanese Culture,* "technical knowledge is not enough. One has to transcend technique so that the art grows out of the unconscious." A central concept of Zen is the idea of "oneness," described by sports psychologist Terry Orlick in his book, *In Pursuit of Excellence,* as "becoming inseparable from the essence of what you are doing each moment...It is being all here, totally present, and absorbing yourself in, totally connecting yourself to...your task...." The idea is that you *become* what you are doing. "The dancer becomes the dance," said author Louis L'Amour, "...I am the writing."

Flow extends our experience beyond what we perceive as our personal limits, and sometimes people are afraid of such an experience. However, to go beyond and to find ourselves enjoying and succeeding at it can strengthen our capacity to motivate ourselves. This is the secret to detaching ourselves from external rewards and punishments and locating within ourselves our discipline and desire to be involved in any task.

Dr. Mihaly Csikszentmihalyi, professor of psychology at the University of Chicago, is credited with the first significant studies of the experience of flow as a universal phenomenon and not something exclusive to practitioners of Zen. He studied people doing what they loved to do, like surgeons, artists, and mountain-climbers. Many others have gone on to apply his work to sports, and to art and music. Dr. Steven Ramsland, executive director of a mental healthcare corporation, has studied the experience of flow in work, across all major job categories. What each of these experts has discovered is that, while flow *seems* to happen spontaneously, there are ways to harness its power and make its emergence more regular and more sustained. Their findings can be applied easily to the educational setting.

Csikszentmihalyi claims in his book, *Flow: The Psychology of Optimal Experience,* that, "people who learn to control inner experience will be able to determine the quality of their lives." It is an invested psychic attention to our goals and skills that ensures that we will maintain our interest and continue to improve. "Flow," he says, "is the way people describe their state of mind when consciousness is harmoniously ordered, and they want to pursue whatever they are doing for its own sake."

Any situation can be transformed into a flow-producing activity by forming it into a meaningful pattern, the rewards of which are intrinsic. Consciousness and meaning originate from within you and are free from the influence of external pressures. It requires a total commitment of your emotions and your will because to make it work *for* you instead of just happening *to* you requires practice and perseverance. Flow appears to be effortless but, in fact, involves discipline. You must learn to form goals, focus your concentration at will, and to tune out distractions. That is why, in earlier chapters, you were given the opportunity to practice these skills. The energy involved has to be channeled for maximum benefit and if *you* decide how and when to channel it, you are more in control. The more skilled you become, the more "effortless" the process will seem.

Again, the notion of control must be clarified here. Control, itself, is not the focus, although it is a goal, just as success is a goal but not a focus. When you concentrate on playing a game, for example, you are more likely to perform at your best and win than if you concentrate on winning. Similarly with flow, if you concentrate on control because you *need* it, you will more likely diminish your performance and lose control, than if you allow control to occur naturally as you gain confidence through practice. Csikszentmihalyi insists that you have to give up the safety of the "comfort zone" and allow yourself to be stretched past self-imposed limits; that means you lose the form of control that actually arises as a result of dependence and insecurity. True control is inner discipline and self-assurance.

Some activities are more likely to produce the experience of flow than others. It is easy to imagine a dancer becoming absorbed in the flow of movement. Doing something that you enjoy makes it more likely that you will become "one" with it with less effort, because you are more likely to make time for it and enter into it with a buoyant, energetic attitude. Nevertheless, flow can become part of other activities too, though it may require more discipline and effort, and possibly a change of attitude.

Psychologist Abraham Maslow, famous for his work with "peak experience," suggests that it is a universal human tendency to strive toward growth, health, and a higher quality of experience. Such goals can be achieved when we become more centered; flow is the result of gaining the sort of focus and purpose needed for becoming centered. With flow, we motivate ourselves to do an activity for the love of doing it, and the activities that we love in a healthy frame of mind are those that will improve our experience. People questioned by Dr. Ramsland who emerge from flow report that their work is of higher quality, and is more creative and satisfying than are the products of more mediocre conditions. They also report a strong desire to experience it again, because it raised their self-confidence, optimism, and enjoyment. They reported feeling "most alive" while engaged at "full throttle."

"Everything seems to go right," said a pipefitter, "and you feel good about yourself and about things in general."

"I have enough energy," said a flight attendant, "that I feel I can give more of myself to others and still not be drained."

In sports, an athlete breaks the pain barrier and reaches a state of euphoric release. In work, people become more involved and enjoy it more. The student can achieve this, too. "Psychologically," says Dr. Ramsland, "flow is the process that is central to all experiences of peak performance."

————————————————————— Flow: The Experience

People who report having experienced flow agree on its qualities. Your mind is alert and focused and, although you are immersed deeply into your task, perception is at crystal clarity. You are "lost" in the experience, yet retain and increase your sense of control. Your inner awareness increases as awareness of externals like noise, odors, and even your bodily distractions diminish. Time seems simultaneously slower and faster: you are so involved it seems as if no time is passing, and yet it seems to have passed faster than you experienced when you look at the clock. There is a heightened feeling of excitement as an easy rhythm develops. Your work seems to flow fluidly and concentration is no longer an effort. Your thoughts and activity harmonize and you open yourself to ideas and perceptions that seem to arise from some mysterious source. Any tools you use become extensions of your body and your attention seems to focus itself. It feels as if you have been climbing up a cliff by your own effort, then suddenly you are pulled up and over. There is a sense of having been transported into a new reality, a leap into another strata of experience.

It is at this level that the tennis ball looks as big as a basketball to focused players. Not only do they claim to be able to see the seams going round and round as the ball approaches, but the ball appears impossible to miss. The mind has slowed even more in its processing speed at the third level of awareness. Nothing at all clutters it. You *experience* yourself fully in your task with a heightened alertness, instead of watching yourself go through the motions, as in passive states. You are simply doing what you are doing. You are not straining, you are allowing yourself to use all of your resources to take you where the energy is released—a place that transforms your "discipline" into a joyful sense of effortlessness.

Although the actual physiology of flow has not yet been documented, it appears to be something like a trance state, although more energetic. You may have experienced the sense of time slowing down that people report in auto accidents or other crisis states. In a way, flow resembles this experience. Your attention is focused and clear, and something like adrenaline seems to be pumping, although not to the degree that occurs in a "fight or flight" experience. It is more of a *relaxed* energy.

In this state, the analytic and evaluative functions of your mind are minimized. You are not *thinking about* what you are doing. There is no calculation, no positive or negative feedback to break your stride or to distance you from your work. You are not restricting yourself with ego pursuits, with fear of failure, or with any other limiting self-images. You have let go of your self-consciousness. You are in touch with the *immediacy* of your work, focused on the present, and released from the hindering influences of obsessions with the past or future.

You now have the freedom and flexibility to perform at your best, whether that performance involves a professional sport, heart surgery, playing chess, typing, perceiving a theoretical structure, or simply learning in a college classroom. The tension and tightness that results from mental judgments is nonexistent—there is no room for it. Your mind is wholly connected to your task. You are as unified with it as you can be. You are tapping energy resources that you had no idea you possessed, and they are working together, harmoniously. There is no "mind" and "body." There is only mindbody—you.

When you are in the state of flow, the task at hand becomes *enjoyable*. That means, for you as a student, that learning becomes fun. It is much like the feeling you had as a child when you were playing. The day zoomed by and you had no other concern except your immediate focus on what you were doing. And you were enjoying it so much that you wanted to run right back out the next day and play some more. This is what learning is like in the state of flow. You want to keep at it. There is no sense of the drudgery of "I have to study," or "Oh no, not another paper." You study or write the paper because you *want* to—in fact, you look *forward* to it! You desire that sense of unity and energy than can happen, similar to athletes who see beyond the pain threshold to the pleasure that awaits them and rewards them for their discipline and preparation. The experience of flow is part of the motivation for achievement that is coupled with a desire for the full development of personal resources, yielding a higher quality of experience than the drive toward achievement alone.

Flow: Self-Assessment

It should be clear that there are a number of emotional and physical components involved in the experience of flow. I have made a list, based on the qualities identified in the research, of what you can look for. Familiarity with this list will not guarantee that you experience flow, because it is not a matter of checking off the items like an airline pilot to see if you have done everything you need to do before a flight. Rather, it can help you to assess whether you have experienced it, and to what degree. Learning to create the conditions for flow will be of little help if you have no idea what the experience is like. You will want to check the list after the fact, however. Avoid stopping yourself to see whether you are "in flow," or you will break your stride and distract yourself.

Mental calmness

There is a stillness about your state of mind, a lack of anxiety, a sense of peace, despite the fact that your mind is at its most productive and alert level of activity. You feel balanced and centered, even though you may be physically charged.

Positive energy flow

The energy seems to come from a limitless source, like an ocean. Your endurance surprises you. You are able to concentrate for hours without being *aware* that you are concentrating.

Sense of ease of effort

Although you are working harder than you work in any other level of awareness, your effort is unstrained. Work seems more like play.

Feeling inspired and creative

Ideas seem to pop up, one after another. Problems that you may have been grappling with seem to solve themselves. You feel as if you can achieve almost anything, and as if you can do things you have never done before.

Clarity of mental vision

You can perceive the sense of some difficult concept with which you previously may have had trouble. You can solve problems more efficiently. You become more involved with your sensory experience. You understand each word of a difficult or high-speed lecture. You are focused.

Intuitive response

You are not mentally examining and calculating your thoughts, but are experiencing more of a balance between word and image. Flow taps your right-brain potential and merges it with left-brain activities.

Alertness

You are fresh and eager to keep going, even if you have already done as much as you thought you could do for that amount of time. You are sitting up and feeling good rather than exhausted.

Sense of joy

You enjoy what you are doing and emerge from flow with a feeling of excitement about the quality of your work. You experience feelings of surprise, wonder, and involvement that you knew as a child.

The Conditions for Flow

According to Dr. Ramsland, flow seems to move through four stages: (1) preparation, or setting up the conditions; (2) onset, when you first begin to experience it; (3) deepening, like a sleep or trance cycle; and (4) emerging back into ordinary consciousness, but with a sense of accomplishment.

The foundation for flow includes a positive attitude, self-image, and physical well-being; developing skills to achieve balance between anxiety and boredom; having clear goals; attending to opportunities; and coordinating external circumstances with flow-enhancing habits.

Attitude

The first thing to realize is that to control your peak moments of optimum performance does *not* mean to force them. You've already learned this. The skill of inner direction is an essential part of flow. The key is learning to concentrate to the point where the effort becomes "effortless." The desire for flow should not become obsessive. What you want to experience is a sense of joy and confidence, not of desperation or tension; but positive feelings come as a result of *getting into* flow, *not* when they are the focus.

Self-image

Your level of performance is directly related to your self image. How you feel about yourself will have a strong influence on how you feel about what you are doing. The exercises in self-awareness can assist you in improving your self-image. If you have no confidence, chances are slim that you will be able to experience flow in a manner that will benefit your pursuit of learning. Conversely, if you are relatively free of self-doubt and can let go of worries and fears, it is likely you will experience this pleasurable absorption on a regular basis. You must be able to trust yourself to your own resources.

Physical well-being

I have already said that to maximize learning potential, you need balance in your life. This means balance in diet, in exercise, in getting enough sleep, in setting your priorities, in work and play. You may still achieve flow even if you eat nothing but hamburgers and fries, and sleep sporadically, and never walk more than half a block to your classroom three times a week. However, eventually, bad physical and mental habits result in either a sluggish mind, or a mind running on nervous energy; neither of these is fertile ground for planting the seeds for flow. To make flow more likely to happen, and to sustain it for longer periods, good health is an essential factor.

Skills

Through research, experts have found that flow is most likely to occur when you are challenged rather than bored, and when you possess the skills to meet the challenge. Setting your sights too low fails to engage your concentration to the degree necessary for flow to occur. On the other hand, setting them too high can result in frustration and anxiety, which hinder the onset of flow. According to Csikszentmihalyi, you need to know what actions are needed and that you can take those actions. You also need to have the ability to concentrate on doing what needs to be done to meet the challenge, which means you need self-motivation skills, perseverance, and discipline.

Visualization exercises can help here. You can use them

to see yourself achieving success, and even to see yourself in a state of flow. Visualization aids concentration and motivation. One way to do this is to make the activity a game. Give yourself self-imposed deadlines, or compete with your own best efforts. Or reframe what you are doing in a new way. You will be more likely to get involved if you view your studies as an important part of your life goals rather than as individual assignments that must be finished just to get them over with.

Clear goals

In order to get into and sustain the experience of flow, there must be some direction to, as well as clear feedback from, the activities in which you are engaged. Clear goals give purpose and meaning to any experience, enhancing satisfaction and pleasure.

Opportunities

The more opportunities you can find for flow-producing activities, the more skilled you will become at recognizing the conditions that make its occurence more likely. You can practice a bit of mental flexibility here. If you fail to see the opportunities, you will fall back into the sort of hit-and-miss experience of flow that makes it seem sporadic and unpredictable. You can turn events into opportunities by looking at them from different perspectives until you find a perspective that motivates you. For example, if you are bored with an assignment on the ethics of animal research, find a way to connect with it that makes it meaningful to you, and therefore more interesting. You can *make* opportunities happen if they do not readily occur to you.

Circumstances

You need to establish habits or rituals that make the experience of flow more likely to happen. Examine your patterns. For example, if you study best in a quiet setting, chances are better for achieving flow if you find such a place than if you go down to the local pizza place to study. If you are more motivated to write at a clear and organized desk than when it is cluttered, make an effort to keep your desk free of clutter. If later afternoon hits you with the need for a nap, arrange your schedule to take a nap, and study at a time when you feel alert.

Before you begin a project, make sure you have everything you need available and ready. If you have to break from your immediate task to go find a dictionary or more paper, you will break the concentration you need. Be organized.

To achieve alertness, confidence, eagerness, and preparedness will not guarantee a state of flow. However, the chances for this experience are far better than if any of these elements were missing.

_____ Application in the Classroom

Listening

During a lecture, flow occurs most often when the subject matter is meaningful to you, and you can understand it. There must be a balance between boredom and anxiety. Meaning is within your abilities. The state of flow frees you from feeling as if you have to take notes verbatim. You are engaged with the subject in a way that gives your focused mind a chance to listen with comprehension. The better you listen in class, the easier it will be to study the subject, and the more context you will have for answering questions on a test, or for organizing your ideas when writing a paper.

Research

There are a number of skills involved in doing research— from reading to using library resources. Getting yourself organized and having the materials you need in one place will make it easier to achieve a state of flow during research. As with listening, an engaged concentration which rendors the subject meaningful will give you a better grasp of it, and will make the need for repetition less likely.

Writing

Like reading, writing comes more easily in a state of flow than when you attempt to force it. One form of writing, called "stream of consciousness" involves flow as an essential ingredient. Even with formal papers, however, you will be surprised how easily you can put words down on a page if you attend to the conditions for flow listed above.

Speaking

Most students are anxious about speaking in front of a class. Anxiety can block the experience of flow. You can use the skills of visualization and inner direction to get yourself prepared for a speech. In doing so, you will discover that preparation enhances your ability to get into the flow of what you are doing. Often, the first moments of anxiety drop away and you are surprised when the words come easily and the speech is over. An experience about which you were anxious can become one that you found pleasurable and exciting.

Discussion

This sort of activity, in or out of the classroom, can be fragmented and thus can hinder flow from happening. However, there are people who actually do their best thinking and talking when they are engaged in debate or asking and answering questions. They find it energizing. It is likely that you will be exposed to many types of discussions, both guided and unguided. How you view these situations will determine whether they are flow-producing activities. The more involved you get, the more meaningful the discussions are, and the more flow-encouraging conditions are present, the more likely it is that you will experience the state of flow.

Problem-solving

You will be faced with problems of every type, and one of the most amazing aspects of flow is the way these problems can get resolved. Often having a problem will put you into a state of worry and stress, which only grips your mind in tension. Learning to relax and to get into flow can reveal solutions to you that you had no idea you could even think of. When people advise you to "sleep on it," they are suggesting that your unconscious can give you a new perspective on the matter. This is just the way flow works. You can break through habitual or constricted ways of working on problems, and come up with otherwise unforeseen solutions to them.

 The Rewards of Flow

In the state of flow, your mind is free to grasp things that you have never before imagined. You are receptive to new ideas, open, eager, and curious. Ideas that have lain dormant, or have been pushed aside by habit or fear, are now unleashed. You may discover talents you were unaware of, simply because you had never given them a chance. And you will feel good, not just because you are accomplishing something effortlessly, but because being in the state of flow simply feels good in itself. And feeling good, you will perform beyond your expectations. Ideas for a paper will fall into place. Your writing pace will improve. Your endurance will be enhanced by a *desire* to keep going. You will be exhilarated at the results. People who participate in studies on flow tend to report high quality work while in that state. That's one reason flow is so exciting.

I have often introduced my students to the art of inner learning prior to getting on with the course's subject matter. When I get to the concept of flow, students find the idea interesting, even exciting, but often do not trust it. In one course, several students decided to give the approach a chance. They gave up their typical style of participating in class and adopted a new one. Instead of thinking about grades, they got involved with the subject. Instead of taking copious notes, they listened actively. The discussions showed a great deal of thinking, rather than just questions for clarification or for some sentence to be repeated. Students were surprised to discover that writing papers *felt* differently to them, and they were not as anxious about the final exam because they were confident about the material. They began to talk with one another about the ideas outside of class, and they were eager to come to class. Their enthusiasm often drew *me* into a state of flow in my teaching, and we were all surprised at how quickly the semester flew by. These students had learned to really *enjoy* their education.

Great performance is motivated from within. External rewards and goals can sustain short-term performance but at the risk of burnout. Knowing your internal motivations and being able to summon them forth is crucial to striving for excellence and self-renewal that the state of flow can help you achieve.

<hr>

Summary

Attending to the experience of flow has been found to be effective across all types of activities for improving quality, performance and enjoyment. A state of flow reduces boredom, anxiety, and frustration, and helps you to achieve a passion for what you are doing. You can experience flow more often and for longer periods of time by understanding the conditions that encourage it. The rewards of flow include long-term motivation that can sustain the art of inner learning not only in your day-to-day activities through four years of college, but also in your chosen career. Graduation does not signal an end, but an exciting beginning.

Exercise _____

Select an academic task like writing a paper or learning a new computer program that will take some time to achieve and one that challenges you. Set up the conditions that will help you to concentrate and give this experience a try. Record the results, then think of other ways to apply it.

Summary of Part 2

- The art of inner learning requires self-awareness, mental flexibility, mental agility, and vision.
- Double reflection can help sharpen and expand self-awareness.
- Mental flexibility is the ability to see more than one perspective; mental agility is the ability to act on a new perspective.
- The technique of visualization, trust of inner direction, and concentration enhance your ability to engage in inner learning.
- Visualization involves the ability to employ vivid images to represent, facilitate, or enhance experiences, skills, and achievements.
- Inner direction is an unself-conscious, uncritical ability to allow yourself to perform in a natural coordination of mind and body.
- Deep concentration involves an ability to achieve a mental stillness that takes you beyond passive, diffuse levels of awareness towards a relaxed but alert focus.
- Mental energy channeled through these techniques can emerge as an altered state of consciousness known as "flow."
- Flow is inner learning performed at its peak, experienced as an effortless, creative, and energetic style of absorption in your activities that yields a sense of joy, satisfaction, and control.
- The stronger and more sustained the experience of flow, the stronger will be the motivation to continue to learn in a manner that facilitates flow.

Solutions to puzzles, p. 147

1. *One* of the coins is not a nickel, but the other one is.
2. Hold it six feet up. It will not break after five feet of the drop, but will when it hits the floor.
3. One hour.
4. The driver knew where to drop her off.
5. The surgeon is his mother.
6. All of them. Any with 31 days have thirty.
7. He's still alive.
8. Of course, between the third and fifth day of the month.
9. Once. After that, the number is twenty-two.
10. It was the spare.

Solutions to Exercises, p. 151

No. 1.

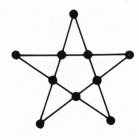

4 in each row
5 rows
10 trees

No. 2.

(Have to go outside the apparent framework)

The Art of Learning

Applications

14

Learning in a College Setting

A student named John once proudly claimed that he had come to college to learn. He viewed this posture as something that set him off from most other students. He was quite intense about attending lectures, sitting in the front of the class, asking questions, taking notes, and studying for exams. He even visited his professor during office hours. He had one problem, however, with his professor's classroom technique. He detested working in groups.

"I have nothing to say to them and they have nothing to say to me," he summed up. He had no respect for his fellow students and felt that group discussions of any kind only wasted valuable time—time the professor should be using to lecture. In short, John wanted to learn only from professors and scholarly authors.

John is not alone in his feelings. There is a great deal of resistance to group work among college students (although not typically as much hostility as John expressed.) Students feel that they will be short-changed in their grades by those in their group who cannot or will not pull their weight. Or they simply believe there is nothing to be gained by the experience.

However, learning does not take place in a vacuum of individual solitude. Nor is it limited to what goes on between a teacher and a student. Just as professors keep adding to their knowledge and skills by developing relationships with colleagues and students, so can students learn from one another. The learning community is made

195

up of individuals and groups of various sizes, from class-room teams to associations of major universities. And just as in all relationships, there may be problems as well as benefits. You may feel pressured to conform and limit your creativity, but you can also be stimulated by the ideas of others and transcend self-imposed limits. Perhaps the best strategy for getting the most from the learning community (while sacrificing the least) is to develop confidence in your own unique qualities and ideas, and retain intrinsic motivation at the same time that you work on flexibility and tolerance in relating to the people around you. (Otherwise you can become blocked in developing inner learning, which is as involved with relationships that facilitate or hinder learning as it is with your individual habits.)

Describing your relationship to the broader community of people associated with your college experience requires careful steps. First, I will talk about you as an individual. Then I will address the benefits and problems of working with groups. Finally, I will describe the balance between being an independent thinker and cooperating with people who can assist you with genuine gains in your learning skills. This chapter will supply the context for a later discussion of applications in a college setting.

—————— Individuality and Independent Thinking

Independent thinking means that you have the ability to develop your own perspective on a situation or problem, and that you can devise your own course of action with regard to that problem. It means first believing that you can break away from the patterned thinking of the "tried and true" and develop opinions and ideas that are *yours* and not someone else's.

Ellyn was excited about a certain theory in physics. She described it to everyone who would listen and encouraged them to read the books she had on the subject. When I asked about her enthusiasm, she told me that she learned about it from a professor. I knew she viewed this person as a mentor and wondered how much of her enthusiasm was really his. Later, when I ran into her again, she was no longer excited. She said she had grown bored with the theory. Further probing revealed that Ellyn had a new mentor who did not agree with the theory.

Being an individual means that you have a unique way of looking at things. Ellyn was blind to how she had formed "her" opinion. Not realizing how prone she was to changing her views to please someone else, she echoed her professor's but continued to claim that the opinions she expressed were hers.

You would probably like to believe that almost everything you think is unique to you—that you are an independent thinker. However, such a belief, ironically, may indicate that you are following the crowd. It is popular in our culture to consider ourselves as "independent thinkers." Many of us are influenced by the people around us or by the media to adopt the language and the facade that gives others the impression that we are independent thinkers. Certainly Ellyn thought this about herself, but it was clear that she was not.

Social influences shape everyone's ideas, sometimes in surprising ways. In a famous experiment, volunteers were asked to compare lines of different lengths drawn on cards. On one card, there was a single line. On another, there were three lines of different lengths. Groups of volunteers were asked to judge which of the three lines most closely corresponded to the length of the single line. For two trials per group, everyone agreed. It seemed obvious which line most clearly matched. The third time around, however, with the same cards, everyone except one person seemed to make an error of judgment. The lone dissenter always disagreed with the others...at first. He or she did not realize that the other "volunteers" were in fact hired to make wrong choices and to try to pressure the single person into agreeing with them—against his or her own perception. In succeeding trials, and with person after person, the dissenter became nervous and was more likely than not to join the majority opinion. Other experiments also confirm that people tend to conform to the voice of the majority, even if they believe the voice is in error. It seems likely, then, that many of our opinions are influenced, at least in part, by what others have said.

Think for a moment about what actually makes you an individual. List everything you can. Then have someone else make a similar list and compare yours to theirs. How similar are they? What does this tell you about the independence of your concept of individuality?

Now look at the clothing that you have on. Are you wearing anything that is currently in fashion? How did you select your clothes? How much time did you really spend thinking through *mindfully* why you bought or dressed yourself in a certain item? How many items of clothing are you wearing that might make you look foolish or conspicuous by fashion standards? What does this say about your independence? What about clothing that you might have chosen in order to appear independent? How similar is it to other people who have the same goal in mind?

Look around you the next time you are in the classroom. How many people are wearing what is currently in fashion? Chances are, the people who appear to you to be conforming to fashion standards set by society consider themselves to be individuals and perhaps even independent thinkers.

You can apply this self-examination to many other things. Think about the music you listen to, the television programs you watch or the movies you attend. Think about habits you have adopted in order to get along with a group of friends.

Much of our behavior is routine and automatic, and is often controlled by our need to be accepted. External forces play off this vulnerability. Newspaper and magazines often tell us what to think, which political candidate to vote for, which bestsellers to buy. You probably know people who jump on every bandwagon in order not to be left out, but you may not realize how prone each of us is to changing our behavior or ideas in order to avoid being conspicuous in an "unacceptable" manner. We tended to imitate others when we were children in order to learn, and these habits stay with us.

It is this imitation that often becomes a blindspot with us, because it is so automatic and became a practice before we became aware of it. With some effort, you can detect some of those patterns.

1. Check out how much you agree with others and how thoroughly you have really thought through your opinions and actions.

2. Do some guided imagery experiments in groups to discover your differences from others, especially from friends. For example, have each person find an object to describe, then compare objects, styles of description, and reasons for selecting the objects. Or have everyone describe an animal they would be, and why.

3. Evaluate the types of decisions you make *before* you consult the opinions of others.

4. Assess your skill of really *listening* to the other sides of issues on which you have formed an opinion. See how often you can detect and acknowledge the reasoning process, even if you do not agree with the final position.

5. Check how often you change your position (or clothing or tastes) just for the sake of giving in to pressure and conforming to what someone else thinks, and list ways that you can have confidence in your own ideas and tastes.

Think about the following situation. Lisa and Alice were working together on a project for their biology course. Whenever Lisa made suggestions, Alice criticized her. Lisa soon did whatever Alice said, feeling that Alice knew more than she did about the subject. Which of them has more confidence?

The answer is that neither has confidence, although they show their weakness in different ways. Lisa allowed herself to be denigrated, and Alice revealed the need to control and undermine. Taking charge does not imply self-confidence, especially if it is done at another person's expense.

True confidence is part of an inner attitude. It is relaxed, assured, and ready for challenge. Having confidence means you have the ability to separate criticism of your ideas from criticism of your person, to discern criticism that is productive from criticism that is destructive, and to turn productive criticism into an opportunity for learning and growth.

Self-doubt often comes from the tendency to believe that others are more intelligent or skilled than we are, that they have a more secure perspective. However, others are as prone to limitations and mistakes as we are. Standards that are "tried and true" may be less secure than you think. Many former traditions have been forced to yield to something better. Most situations allow room for multiple perspectives, and yours may be as valid as someone else's. At the very least, your ideas deserve to be heard. It is even possible that you could teach your teachers a thing or two!

However, being an independent thinker sometimes means that you will be challenged. There will always be people looking to blame or criticize others, or take them down a peg or two. Confidence will help you to resist more effectively than defensiveness.

To build confidence, make a list of qualities about yourself that you like. You may wish to refer to Chapter 7 to help you with specifics. Meditate on these qualities, or on how you can improve them, until you perceive yourself as a person with some degree of power. Visualization can assist you.

When you feel as if you can value yourself as an individual and that you can have confidence in offering your ideas, you will fare better in the interactive process.

 The Interactive Process

A student who wanted to be a writer shunned creative writing classes because they often required one to read one's work in front of the class. She was not going to put herself and her extreme self-consciousness on the line in front of other students. She did not believe there was anything to gain, or that the potential gains would outweigh the humiliation.

Another student had similar aspirations. She did take a creative writing course, despite her desperate shyness. It was tough at first, but she stuck it out. Not only did she receive an excellent grade for her work, but her personality literally blossomed. She received both praise and criticism, but so did all of the other students, and she discovered that the class attention was not focused exclusively on her (a central feature of self-conscious fears.) Her writing improved because she began to understand what interested other people, what hindered their comprehension of her work, and what really grabbed them. She grew more confident about her abilities to communicate. These are essential skills for any aspiring writer to develop. The student who shunned these opportunities might have protected her self-image, but she missed out on getting important feedback that could enable her to develop her aspirations.

There is an interconnectedness in the college setting which may be difficult to perceive at first. Courses are listed as distinct subject areas. Professors specialize, sometimes to the extent that even their closest colleagues fail to understand them. Yet among subject areas, as among scholars, there are themes and values that pull many apparently disparate elements together.

A single perspective on an issue or subject area is limited. To illustrate, imagine that you are looking at a large building. You can see only one side. It is brown. So you would describe a brown building. However, suppose the building is brown only on the side you see. Then your conclusion would be false. You need another perspective. You will have to move around the building and see it from all sides before you can give an adequate characterization.

Yet the ability to see all sides of something is not always possible. That is why another person's perspective can be valuable. Other perspectives broaden and deepen our own understanding by giving us a vantage point that may otherwise be inaccessible to us.

When Janet was an undergraduate, one of her professors offered extra sessions for anyone who wanted to learn more. Typically about six to eight students would show up. All were prepared and eager, and each one had a unique perspective on how to interpret the material that they were reading. The discussions were fruitful and often exciting. It was in these small groups that Janet learned to shrug off her self-consciousness and contribute. Sometimes she made ordinary remarks that did not impress anyone, but neither did it result in criticism. Once in awhile, she would say something that touched off a new and stimulating course of discussion. She learned a lot, not only "information," but also about sharing in a community of minds. When she transferred to another school, she had visions of more roundtable discussions in which informed, serious students would enthusiastically participate.

To her great amazement, very little of this kind of discussion materialized, and she felt cheated. She had books and access to the professor, but what she lacked was the opportunity to broaden her perspective with the ideas of others who were working in the same subject area. Janet emerged from her program with a degree, but also with the feeling that she had received less of an education than she could have received had others recognized the value of group discussions.

Students who view group discussions negatively, the way that John did in the example that opened this chapter, are not only missing out on the potential contributions that can be gained from listening to others, but they are also depriving fellow classmates of their own perspectives. If I see the brown side of a multicolored building, and you see the red side but fail to inform me of your perspective, then my distorted impression of the building is as much a function of your "can't be bothered" attitude as it is of my own limitations. Together we can get a little closer to truth, and gain the benefits of mutual cooperation.

The classroom is an organic whole. It is not just a loose collection of individuals sitting at so many desks, with a professor in front. It is a place where the energy of many minds can surge together and *create* a mutually beneficial outcome. Separate minds working alone cannot produce the brainstorming session that members of a unified group can produce. World-changing theories of quantum physics have actually been derived from such sessions.

Learning is give-and-take. If you withhold your contribution, you deprive others of what your efforts and ideas may have helped them to achieve in coordination with their own, just as they can deprive you. What emerges from such a session depends on each person, and the outcome may be only a shadow of what it could be if everyone participates. You cannot help what others will or will not do, but you can help what *you* do. If you sit back and avoid your part in the energy flow of contributing minds, you risk, at the very least, retaining an inaccurate sense of the subject. There is a point at which a group can become as strong as its strongest member, but that group must first work together as a cohesive team coordinated by a common goal.

Remarkably creative work can come from students who have decided to make the most of the group situation. When they cooperate, they can surpass the learning opportunities available to them from lectures and exercises. For example, when a group pulls together to help one of its members whose skills are poor, they not only improve their chances for a better grade, but they learn valuable teamwork skills which will help them perform better in the working world.

When you find yourself in a group situation, you will respond and react just the way you would to any social context. That is, you will find that there are people you like and there are people you dislike. Some people are irritating, some exploit, some manipulate, some act helpless. Some will be eager and bright, while others need more time to understand a problem. You will have choices. You can walk away (even if it means jeopardizing your grade,) or you can try to make the most of a situation.

One student by the name of Barry, never addressed a question or an issue directly, yet he loved to talk consistently. It was difficult to think about squelching his enthusiasm, yet it was also clear that the other students were growing more irritated with his irrelevant chatter. Rather than putting Barry on the spot and embarrassing him, several other students began to try to see the class through Barry's eyes. Soon they viewed his "disturbances" with a sense of humor, and even with compassion. Barry responded to their gentle proddings. He still continued to talk off the subject, but he began to sense his connection to others in the classroom and to be sensitive to his own tendency to dominate. He learned, but so did the other students. While they picked up academic information, they also learned a great deal about effective human interaction.

It is a valuable talent in working in groups—extending even to the class as a whole—to be able to see through the eyes of another person. It diminishes prejudice and irritation, and increases sensitivity. Increased sensitivity facilitates your learning energies. You are struggling *together* as a group, rather than attempting to step on one another to make it to the top of the heap.

There is always risk involved in a group. Will everyone do their share? Sometimes this fear defeats the group. If one person shows distrust or unwillingness, it has a negative psychological effect on the others. Soon no one trusts anyone else and the work does not get done. Group cohesiveness depends on group solidarity. The more cohesive a group, the more likely it is that each member will be productive and respectful of the others.

The "They"

A group of people can provide an opportunity to broaden the learning experience. However, they can also become the greatest stumbling block. The "they" is a social force. It is the group pressure to conform. The term comes from Heidegger's philosophical description of one of the most insidious forces we encounter in our day-to-day existence. Neutral and impersonal, the "they" inconspicuously dominates what we think, how we feel, what we talk about, how we dress, what we read, and what opinions we have. The list is as long as the activities we pursue. The "they" encourages us to be average, to act like the norm and to strive for the same goals. People are pressured to imitate one another and suppress their individuality and independence.

Anthony was in his first year of medical school. He took a course in which the professor mumbled and seemed incoherent. The other students complained among themselves about their inability to learn from this man. Most of them stopped going to class and resigned themselves to getting nothing from the course.

Anthony felt the pressure to conform. In order to be "one of the guys," he adopted their attitude and joined them in their negativism. He recognized, however, that he was getting dragged down needlessly. He decided to go ahead and attend the classes and to go to each of the slide shows the professor had assigned. He made up his mind to resist the pressure from his classmates to shrug off the professor, and at the end of the course, he was glad. He felt he had learned a great deal. His classmates, however, had learned nothing and they blamed it on the professor.

The pressure Anthony experienced was the group's influence to diffuse personal responsibility: "If we all feel this way, then no one of us is to blame for not learning." Each person sees himself or herself in others. That is, being average and having no significant ideas, relationships, or responsibilities is construed as the ideal. The goal is to maintain the status quo and have no one become independent enough to "rock the boat." Peer pressure makes you less rather than more, while *seeming* to make you someone special in virtue of "being accepted."

Take a few minutes to think about how social pressure influences your own life. Have you ever given in? Think about why.

Under the influence of the "they" creativity is minimized and constructive dialogue is kept to a minimum. We get to know one another through *what is said about* the other rather than by really caring about and listening to the concerns of the other. The "they" creates a filter through which we relate to one another, and cultivates the fertile soil for disconcerting psychic distances that often occur among classmates. We push people away so as to more easily keep up the "right" appearances.

Responsibility for learning requires courage to step out

and be your own person. To think your own thoughts. To study when others party. To attend class when others pressure you to think of it as a waste of time. To reap rewards that others may ridicule. In short, daring to take initiatives separate from those of the group can be advantageous to your learning experience.

--------------------- Finding the Balance: An Exercise

To this point, you have been invited to think about what it means to be individual, as well as what it means to work within the structure of a group. Both forms of learning have a negative and a positive side, and it is hard to draw the line at where one begins and the other ends.

In groups, the direction will depend on the attitudes of those involved. One motivated person can inspire the others. Even when there are group members who will not pull their own weight, those who do want to get something from the experience, can. The trick is to use self-confidence to resist the negative energy of group pressures and to make up your mind to actively pursue the benefits that can be reaped.

You can try this out by forming a study group. As part of the process of getting to know each other and how well you might work together, have everyone attend the same lecture or film, or have each person read the same section of a text and take notes on what they viewed as the important points. Then get together and compare notes. Have everyone write about their perception of the group's strengths and weaknesses as a team, along with suggestions for improvement. The suggestions should include individual self-assessments in relation to the group to indicate what each person believes he or she can contribute. The next step is to apply this analysis to a genuine assignment.

The best groups include individuals who value and use their own talents to work with others toward a goal. They are neither intimidated by, nor resistant to, other opinions. They do not perceive their uniqueness as threatened, and they respect the uniqueness of other members. They can think independently without having to withdraw into solitary activity, and they recognize the value and benefits of cooperation. Being an individual is not negated by participation in a group because the group works best when individuality is respected. The balance lies between the tension of being oneself and cutting oneself off from the group, vs. being *in* a group and being *devoured* by it. It may be tricky to decide whether stating an opinion not generally accepted within a group is an exercise of independent thinking or the expression of a self-absorbed, self-deceived person. There is no formula for measuring it. However, self-confident individuals are not afraid to listen to others and admit the possibility of being blind to personal traits that can hinder the group. People who can listen without fear of losing their own perspective are people who will understand the balance between unproductive individuality and succumbing to "the they." Students who utilize the art of inner learning have an advantage in self-awareness and self-mastery.

_____ Summary

The classroom is an organic system, made up of both mental and physical energies, and of individual and group perspectives. It is part of a larger learning community. The more the energy is channeled toward educational goals, the greater the potential for learning. Negative energy is stifling and results in unproductive psychic distances, along with harmful, mediocre competition that neutralizes quality in performance. Positive energy, derived from self-confidence, a will to learn, and a sensitivity and respect toward others as mutual partners in the classroom situation, can gather into stimulating brainstorming that makes the whole far greater than the sum of its parts. Within the larger community you *can* find a place and better develop your personal learning skills.

15

Inner Learning: Applications

The reasons for developing the art of inner learning are related specifically and personally to you as the learner, even in a group. Inner learning is not meant just to help you get through college, with all its pressures, but to teach you a way of life that will make your experiences more satisfying and meaningful. If you decide to make a commitment to using inner learning as a general approach to your studies, you will discover that it yields many advantageous benefits:

1. Self-knowledge
2. Inventiveness/resourcefulness
3. Self-formed interests and motivations
4. Eagerness for the future
5. Satisfaction in personal achievement
6. Appreciation for your time and efforts
7. Lack of boredom
8. Alert involvement
9. Youthful spirit
10. Flexible perspective/adaptability
11. Openness to opportunities
12. Desire to transcend past standards and performances
13. Urge toward self-realization
14. Experience with peak performance
15. Motivation to keep learning
16. Self-confidence

A look into the future appears to favor opportunities for people who take an active rather than passive approach to learning, and who can involve themselves in whatever they do with a sense of purpose, direction, satisfaction, and an ability to envision and offer solutions to problems. Developing these traits in college will not only assist you in your daily challenges, but will also prepare you to face with confidence what lies ahead.

—————————— Inner Learning and Personal Direction

While you have been shown the techniques of inner learning in a general way, and how it can assist you in the learning community as a whole, it is important that you also understand how to apply them to your personal situation. Getting yourself more involved and committing yourself to being alert will not be of much use unless you have a specific purpose and direction.

Purpose, of course, means that you have some reason to be in college and some reason to develop yourself into a more effective learner. Whatever your purpose, your direction will take the form of the steps needed to achieve your goals. How can the art of inner learning help?

Going back to the beginning with your more self-aware and skilled perspective, reassess your learning style from Chapter 1, along with your values. Did you choose your goals or did someone else choose them for you? Are you a self-starter or do you rely on external systems of reward and punishment? Do you tend to be carried along or do you think through the steps you take and the actions you perform? Have you been making any changes?

Becoming more actively and intelligently involved with who you are is the part of inner learning that orients you internally instead of externally, and does so actively, with interest in what self-knowledge means. This generalizes to setting goals and deciding on directions. The more inner-directed you are in one area, the more likely you will be able to recognize the benefits for other areas.

Also, self-knowledge assists you in the *process* of selection necessary for setting goals and directions. You know best what you like, what you want to find out more about, what skills you have or want to develop. If you get sick at the thought of blood, you probably will not go into the medical field. If you grow enthused at the idea of helping people, perhaps you will consider social work instead of mathematics. That is, knowing yourself can help you to set your own directions and avoid being directed by someone else. As you make your own choices, you exercise more control over your life, especially if your choices are made with the strong component of self-awareness that can separate whim from true motivation.

The art of inner learning may also involve you with a mentor who can help you to deepen your knowledge or skill in a subject area. If you are actively engaged in the classroom, you may relate well to a particular professor. Only if you are alert to the present as you learn, and involved in the teacher-student relationship as a partnership will you understand what a mentor can do for you.

True mentors are only guides. They do not attempt to control you or make decisions for you, but only offer suggestions from the perspective of their experience and expertise. They do not seek disciples who become dependent on them or boost their egos, nor would they allow a student to enter into this sort of arrangement. They work within a fiduciary relationship, but it is usually more intense and more personally significant for the student. Mentors care about the student as a person whose future they wish to follow. Students who experience this sort of personal attention may gain career advantages and advice that can help to establish and strengthen their directions. Students, however, must be careful not to become dependent or allow their mentor to do their thinking for them.

If you have a mentor, the art of inner learning offers you another device for assisting yourself in your achieving, step-by-step, the goals you set. You can even conjure up the image of a mentor—someone who is the model for you for what you want to achieve, but who may not be physically available. For example, theater students may visualize working with a professional actor who exhibits for them the epitome of their craft. Budding artists may look to the style of a particular painter or sculptor. In any area there will be a hero figure who exemplifies through actions, thoughts, or inventions, the goals toward which you want to strive.

The experience of flow, itself, can guide you toward anchoring yourself in a particular subject, skill, or goal. If you discover that you are better able to become absorbed in one subject area over others, you may decide to pursue that interest rather than one in which you have trouble involving yourself.

Finding your direction and developing purpose in your life demands that you think for yourself. Inner learning involves the sort of alert mental activity and self-awareness that makes independent thinking not only more likely but essential.

Inner Learning and College Skills

Although the art of inner learning is, itself, a family of skills, it is primarily a way to channel physical energy and mind/body coordination. As such, it can be used in learning and improving other skills. There are many books for college students on the market that offer strategies for study skills and classroom techniques, but many of them can be approached through either extrinsic or intrinsic motivating systems. Research shows that people who develop inner learning skills not only report being more effective in what they do, but also enjoy it more. You can benefit in the same ways by approaching specific skills and tasks through inner learning.

Taking notes

The current educational system relies heavily on dispensing information and you are expected to record what your professors say as accurately and comprehensively as possible. This results in anxiously scribbling everything you hear, without grasping the material as it goes into your notebook. With inner learning you are attuned to the present moment so that your focused mind is better able to listen for imporant material, comprehend it as it is offered, and take notes more strategically—with less work later in trying to figure out what you wrote and to memorize it. You are less anxious, less worried about your grade, and more interested in understanding. You ask questions as they occur to you because you are engaged with the material in a way that allows you to know immediately whether you understand it or need clarification. Your concentration is undivided; you are not watching the time and missing material as you become distracted. The strategies offered in college study guides are easier to master, and you may even devise your own.

Reading Texts

You have probably experienced the frustration of reading through several pages of complex material only to realize that you cannot remember anything that you just read. Inner learning minimizes this problem because your mind is focused, alert, able to concentrate, comprehend, and place the material into a context that is easier to understand and remember, without having to rely on superficial memorization. You have a purpose in reading a text that is personally meaningful to you rather than simply reading an assignment for a class. You are better able to immediately grasp whether the material is too difficult, and to formulate questions about it. You are motivated to read the material for what it offers you, and to ask the questions that will assist you in understanding. You will also be motivated to do exercises on your own, even if they are not assigned, simply because you want to learn and not just "get by."

Listening

With inner learning, you become self-aware and better able to realize the ways in which you sabotage yourself from becoming a member of the learning community. As you realize the value of listening to other perspectives, you begin to develop the habit of concentrating on what others say and to really hear them, rather than just acknowledging that they are talking, or shielding yourself from their opinions. Active, alert, and focused concentration, without self-conscious barriers offers you immediate comprehension that not only makes you a better listener, but a person more likely to be able to engage in a discussion or debate without diverging from the issue or becoming defensive.

Interacting with professors

Students who take a passive approach to their learning are often too insecure about their grasp of the subject to approach a professor to discuss ideas or ask questions. Students who engage in active, intrinsically motivated learning are more confident that they can engage in a conversation about a subject because they have a more holistic grasp of the material and have a better sense of the points that they need clarified. Self-awareness and the possession of a sense of purpose generates self-confidence and the ability to approach professors without hesitation. Students also come to realize that learning is not merely contained in the classroom and assignments, but can be gained in after-class discussions as well. Such students are more motivated to seek these kinds of opportunities than are those who believe that classroom exposure is "adequate," or who do not think beyond superficial, external goals. Inner learners also realize that professors are not to blame for their own performance.

Communicating

Learning is not just a matter of filling your mind with information but it is a way of processing that information in order to come up with your own ideas on it and to make contributions to further the field of knowledge. To do that, you must be able to communicate in discussions, arguments, speeches, or in writing. The alert, focused, self-reliant and self-motivated person has an immediate grasp of the material and can place it in a personally relevant context. This person also has an advantage in discussing the material over one who has to sort through notes and memorize information before talking about it. Having goals and directions that go beyond short-range achievements like "getting an A in geology" enables a person to explore and possibly provoke new directions and aspirations, as well as acquire the motivation to be organized and clear.

_____ Inner Learning and Independent Thinking

You have learned what it means to be involved in a community of learners. You now understand that learning is not a solitary activity, and that involvement offers real benefits. You are also aware, however, that groups can try to crush your individuality with manipulation or pressure. To think independently from a group in which you are involved, whether it is an assigned group in a course, a class, or the entire academic community, takes courage. The art of inner learning offers resources.

Being more inner than outer-directed, you possess self-awareness about your strengths and vulnerabilities. Knowing them and working with them can help you achieve confidence, which in turn demands respect from others. Feeling respected, you will have the courage to say what you think. And your thoughts will be more reflective than those of people who participate mindlessly in their education.

Along with active evaluation skills and creativity, the art of inner learning gives you techniques to help you to believe that thinking independently will assist you in your goals and will have a positive effect on your achievements. Visualization, inner direction, and concentration can help you to know your own mind and give you the confidence you need to express yourself. You may also become more creative.

_____ Inner Learning and Creativity

"What feeling, knowledge, or will man has," said Kierkegaard, "depends on the last resort upon what imagination he has."

There is a great deal of concern these days among people in the field of education that traditional styles of classroom instruction have not only failed to encourage creativity, but have actually stifled it. This may have serious social, economic, and cultural effects.

"I maintain," said psychologist Carl Rogers,

> that there is a desperate social need for the creative behavior of creative individuals...Many of the serious criticisms of our culture and its trends may best be formulated in terms of a dearth of creativity...In education we tend to turn out conformists, stereotypes, individuals whose education is "completed," rather than freely creative and original thinkers.

People often believe that creativity is reserved for those with extraordinary talent and that only a privileged few possess it. Yet this trait actually belongs to all of us, in varying degrees. To be creative does not necessarily mean to be able to paint a masterpiece, to write a novel, or to make a world-changing scientific discovery. Nor does it mean you have to be highly intelligent or even knowledgeable. Einstein, who possessed both knowledge and imagination, said that imagination was the more important of the two. According to creativity specialists, creativity is the ability to utilize challenge to envision and effectively adapt to change, or to make the changes yourself. It means going beyond the superficial or habitual to come up with a unique idea or approach—in other words, developing mental agility. You see ways to do something differently, or see several ways to achieve the same goal so that you can compare and choose more effectively. You *play* with the ideas, rather than just accept what tradition or another person tells you.

"Creativity will be a survival skill of the nineties," says psychologist Ellen McGrath. Managers from the smallest companies to the largest corporations are actively seeking resourceful thinkers for important positions. Following in ruts is not impressive. It may get you an A in a traditional classroom, but few people in the post-college world will care about the A if you cannot demonstrate independent and inventive thinking. Although you are generally pressured in society and in school to conform, great discoveries and inventions were developed by people who were able to resist such pressures and think mindfully, for themselves.

Creative minds have the ability to fantasize, to ask, "What if?" When confronted with the need for change, they transform the world around them if they can, or transform themselves if they can't. They can tolerate ambiguity in order to see if there is more than one way to think about or resolve a situation, or to attack a problem. They can readily improvise. The focus is on the process more than the solution, because they find the process rewarding and satisfying. Creative people are concerned with "getting there," of course, but they want to find a way to do so that will involve their skills and push them beyond limits: they want to experience the surprise and delight of the unexpected, and of seeing how something new works out.

Inner learning allows a person to become more creative, because an alert and interested mind is a key element. Passive minds are not focused enough, nor involved enough to engage personal resources in the search for a creative solution or change to a given situation. Nor do they care enough. Creativity comes easily to people who are sufficiently preoccupied with and committed to a problem to focus on it intently until a solution is found. They can more easily get into flow—the state in which people tend to report more creative insight—but at the very least, they are more likely to seek opportunities for creative resolution than is the person who merely acknowledges a situation at a more superficial level of awareness. Visualization also enhances one's ability to see beyond traditional approaches and try out something new.

The creative process involves several steps:

1. First, you must know something about the challenge before you, because the direction you take will typically involve a purpose or goal.

2. Then you must digest the information and really think it through; do not just have an acquaintance with it, as with rote learning.

3. Then, it often helps to let it go. This stage is controversial, but many creative people swear by it—calling it the period of "incubation." The idea is to divert your mind from the task at hand by going for a walk, for example, or by listening to music, similar to the way you allow inner direction to take place. Sometimes people fear that "letting go" will risk losing insight of what they have to do, and might mean starting all over again, and possibly overlooking something that they had already worked out. Usually however, the last stage—inspiration—comes to the relaxed mind.

4. Inspiration. Inspiration seems to bubble up from the unconscious. Puzzles are solved, ideas are synthesized, plots are resolved. It takes you by surprise.

5. Once you have an idea, implement it.

To make creativity more likely, the mind must work at its peak. It must be active, focused, prepared, relaxed, curious, committed, confident, searching for knowledge and allowed to work things out in its own way—all descriptions of inner learning.

Summary

The art of inner learning has many benefits, both in and out of the classroom. To be most effective, it needs to be applied toward specific goals, such as assisting students to develop purpose and direction, to sharpen basic skills, to think independently and to become more creative. Each of these activities is possible with traditional methods of learning, but the art of inner learning enhances the activities by increasing self-awareness, visualization, personal meaning, and active, self-motivated involvement.

Exercises _____

1. Review your list from Chapter 1 and go over each item, describing how inner learning might be beneficial to you in each situation.

2. Visualize yourself making changes.

3. Think of other applications for inner learning in your college situation or in your life.

"There is a learner within you, able and confident, waiting to function freely, usefully and joyfully."
—*Marilyn Ferguson*

16

Becoming a Master

It is time to summarize all that you have become acquainted with in this book. There are many ideas to keep straight, some of which seem at first to contradict others until you have a good grasp of them. You may be feeling a bit confused, but keep in mind that this approach is a tool that, like any tool, takes some time to get used to. Hopefully you have taken advantage of suggestions for interacting with the information in the text so that the ideas and exercises made sense as you went along. The process may be gradual, but the more often you utilize inner learning, the more clearly you will see what it can do for you. Becoming a "master" is a concept from Zen that means achieving inner calmness and self-control. The more mastery you achieve, the more benefits will be released to you through your own learning potential.

The Initial Stages

You can either harm yourself or help yourself with getting the most from your college education. Unfortunately, you can harm yourself without even realizing it. The current educational system, from grade school through college, aims toward getting you through the external demands of the learning process, but offers little organized effort to address the inner dynamic of self-motivation, self-awareness and active, creative involvement. The art of being a student—of developing a learning style that begins within yourself—has been neglected. That makes it more difficult for you to detect how you may be blocking yourself from learning.

To get the most out of college, you must first realize that your degree does not signify the end of your learning career, even though it often symbolizes the end of your formal education. You will benefit by viewing your college experience as a unique and sustained opportunity to practice a lifetime skill. The more effort you devote to it during these early stages, the less effort you will need to expend as later situations arise. It is important to realize that much of the responsibility for your education lies with you.

Your first responsibility is to decide on your purpose in choosing to pursue a college degree and develop ways to sustain the motivation you will need to achieve the goals that are defined by that purpose. Get to know your values. The more personally meaningful your purpose and values are, the more motivated you will be to take each step toward the goals. This may be intimidating because taking such decisions into your own hands makes you accountable for them. However, only by exercising choice and a sense of becoming master of your destiny will your purpose take on the significance required for commitment.

Second, you must understand what is involved on your side of the learning partnership. Your professors have responsibilities, but so do you. The relationship will work best when both parties are fully involved, but you can still gain benefits for yourself even if you are putting more into it. Recognizing and adapting to challenge is part of the art of inner learning, and you will do better to work through difficulties than to give up.

Once you realize that active involvement is required of you, you have some work to do to prepare yourself on several levels: mechanically, mentally and emotionally. You will have to discover and develop the style of learning that will work best for you. The methods advocated in this book move you away from the traditional approach that tends to take authority for yourself away from you and to result in mostly short-term benefits through extrinsic rewards. Whatever long-term benefits it offers are also available with inner learning, an approach that offers more in terms of satisfaction, intrinsic motivation and generalizable, holistic skills.

Inner learning begins with self-awareness, which can be developed with techniques like double reflection that get you to go beyond just observing your personality traits to really *experiencing* them, making them more vivid. As you become more aware of yourself, you will have a better grasp of how your traits and values affect your style of learning.

Having a style involves physical energy, and that energy can be channeled into either positive or negative directions. Those traits that hinder your ability to learn easily and naturally are made more clear with self awareness so that you can work to change them; those that help are also revealed and can be strengthened and used effectively as a source for creating a positive, unselfconscious and confident manner. Hindrances to learning that originate outside yourself can be overcome with an attitude of perseverance and resourcefulness.

The idea is that you must learn to build a relationship with yourself that will allow you to begin to trust yourself to learn in a manner to which you have probably never before been exposed. Finding an inner sense of control and calmness will not only help you to accept your ego-vulnerabilities and work with them, but will also ensure that inner learning becomes a way of life, applicable to any situation, and not just an effective tool for mastering your education in the classroom. Inner learning means getting in touch with a natural, self-generated thirst to learn, and to discover and develop the most effective, enjoyable, and self-renewing way of quenching that thirst.

_____ Reviewing the Technique

It may seem strange to work on exercises for getting to know yourself only to be told that the essence of inner learning is to forget yourself, but both are important to the success of the approach. The idea is to prepare yourself in order to "forget" yourself more effectively, and for that you need to know how you respond and react to various situations. However, being aware of your personality traits does not mean to become self-absorbed, which would, itself, be another learning hindrance. In order to learn to develop mental flexibility, agility, and trust for your own resources, you must know how you might block or facilitate them. So to know yourself in order to be able to forget yourself is not really as strange as it seems.

Inner learning does not focus on goals but on process, like runners who attend to running rather than winning in order to perform at their best; they make their chances for winning even greater. Watching the goal is like evaluating yourself: it becomes an interference, attaching weights to your feet. You become so wrapped up in *trying* to win that you neglect the process that allows your inner resources to coordinate and help you to achieve your best performance. So you develop goals in order to have direction and motivation, but you allow yourself to lose sight of them in order to concentrate on the pursuit. This is like selecting a major to help you to organize your course load, but then forgetting about the end results while you concentrate on learning.

One of the most important skills involved in the art of inner learning is to be able to shut down your critical awareness of what you are doing and just do it. Being too aware, especially in preparation to judge what you are doing as "good" or "bad" becomes an interference in the smooth flow of just involving yourself in the immediacy of your experience. You may force yourself, try too hard, and thus become tense or anxious. You may expect too much or too little of yourself, creating errors in the way you envision what you can do and thus ensuring that those errors will happen, like a self-fulfilling prophecy. Or you may diminish your opportunity to experience the fullest joy and satisfaction that happens in the immediate moments of concentration and achievement.

You can trust that the potential exists within you to do

your best without having to force yourself or to strain to make it happen. Don't think about what can stop you. Your true capability may yet be untapped, and if you allow yourself to believe that, rather than believing that you know exactly what your limitations are, you may be as surprised as athletes who see the ball out of range, but reach out anyway and catch or hit it. When something blocks you, trust that your mind will work out a way to meet the challenge. Chances are better that it will if you allow it to than if you become stressed out over the possibility that you can't.

There are no guarantees, but there *are* ways to make success more likely. Tension is like building a dam on a river for no reason other than to block the flow of water. Get in touch with the natural coordination of your mind and body. Let yourself know what you want of your resources, then let go and do it.

The initial effort that you will have to bring to bear to learn this approach may seem like a lot of work, but that is partly because you are "unlearning" other habits. It will be like working against gravity. You need perseverance and commitment—doing it because it's what you want. You will also need to be careful not to revert to old habits in the guise of the new approach. For example, you may become so concerned with learning the inner art that you become critically aware of how well or how badly you are doing—which just defeats the effort. The art of inner learning relies as much on trusting yourself and letting go in order to engage in *the art* it does in utilizing that skill to learn other subjects. You may become frustrated, then worried and perhaps even discouraged that it is not "working" for you. However, those are the signs that you are not just allowing yourself to engage in the natural process of inner learning.

Let go of being too aware of yourself doing something. Inner learning can become like breathing or walking. If you tried to instruct yourself in walking, becoming aware of moving each muscle and of coordinating your hands and feet, you would probably become quite clumsy. Doing something like walking is accomplished through inner direction, in which the mind and body coordinate with each other to achieve movement easily, without the need for conscious verbal instruction. Such activity bypasses ego-centered awareness, like playing a musical instrument as if it were part of us, rather than thinking about each note before it is played.

You may fear the loss of control that can happen when you trust a process you do not consciously direct. You are required to surrender. However, this form of surrender actually gives you control, but *you* deliver the control to your inner resources. You actually possess an inner knowledge of how to do things, especially after you have performed them a few times. This inner knowledge can move you more surely toward your goals than "head" knowledge that is cluttered with worry, self-doubt or critical judgments.

Visualization can assist the inner process by giving you a sense of direction, by encouraging you to see yourself taking each step successfully, and by delivering to you a vivid *feel* of the experience of achieving both ultimate and process goals. Using images will help you to understand why a still, relaxed mind, uncluttered by distractions, more effectively engages you in progressively more focused concentration. The deeper the concentration, the more you will forget yourself, forego "trying" and just *do*.

At this point, you may or may not experience flow, the total absorption in what you are doing—the moment of wholeness—that can accompany deep concentration. There are things you can do to make it more likely to occur than not, but no amount of desire or effort will bring it about. It happens as a result of the right degree of concentration and involvement. You disappear into your activity, lose track of time, shut out distractions and emerge to a feeling that you have performed at your peak. Having forgotten yourself, you have also forgotten your self-imposed limitations, judgments and concerns, and your inner potential may have come through to surprise you with what you have done. And having experienced flow, your body stores it as a memory, giving you even better odds of achieving it again, partly because trusting yourself and surrendering has paid off. You will be exhilarated by the quality of this spontaneous experience and, since it happened in the context of the activity of learning, you will want to experience it again. Flow feeds your self-motivation to learn, becoming a rewarding part of the art of inner learning. What you learn from this experience at its most intense is that you *are* the process of inner learning. *You* are the center. Just as a tool that you learn well seems to become an extension of yourself, so does learning, and it will become more natural, the more you allow it to work with you.

_____ Review of General Benefits

The art of inner learning is similar to what happens when people learn a foreign language. They see it applied and listen to it spoken, then gradually allow it to become a natural part of their orientation to a culture. Their counterparts, who learn the same language by learning grammatical rules and lists of words, will never achieve the same fluency; even if they learn to speak that language effectively and clearly, it will entail much more mental effort.

In the classroom, the difference between these approaches should become apparent to you. For example, if you are learning the basic errors of reasoning in a course on critical reasoning, you may be confronted with a list of these errors to memorize. Instead of memorizing them, if you work on learning them by applying them to actual situations, you will recognize them more easily and have to expend less effort studying for an exam. The list will become a natural part of your perspective as you evaluate someone else's arguments. Were you only to memorize the errors, you might have to consult your list over and over, at the risk of losing sight of what you were evaluating for errors, and you might still never really master an understanding of those errors or an ability to detect them. Your "learning" will be limited to responding to the demands of the course and you may not see how the skill goes beyond that course. Or if you see it, you may not be able to apply the skill for long.

Like any tool, inner learning gives you a way of achieving something. You will still need information and instruction, but you will become more focused on the instruction, allowing your relaxed, alert mind to grasp and absorb it, rather than memorizing and storing it as mere information. *That* is the idea behind inner learning—to bring into your inner resources the information that will broaden your knowledge and develop your skills in a way that provides long-term and practical benefits. You will learn what you want to learn, more fully and more meaningfully; you will become more self-reliant and more energetic about your learning; and you will be setting up conditions that can make your life in and out of the classroom more fulfilling and more satisfying.

Bibliography

The bibliography is categorized by subjects to relate the research to specific chapters. At times, one book applied to more than one chapter, but I placed it the category in which it best fit.

Visualization/Mental Agility

Buzan, Tony. *Use Both Sides of Your Brain.* New York: E. P. Dutton, 1974.

Lazarus, A. A. *In the Mind's Eye: The Power of Imagery for Personal Enhancement.* New York: Guilford, 1984.

"Enhancing Human Performance: Issues, Theories and Teachngs." National Research Council. 1988.

Zilbergeld, Bernie, and Lazarus, Arnold. *Mind Power.* New York: Ivy Books, 1987.

Flow/Excellence/Peak Performance/Concentration

Csikszentmihalyi, Mihaly. *Flow: The Psychology of Optimal Experience.* New York: Harper & Row, 1989.

Dillard, Annie. *Pilgrim at Tinker Creek.* New York: Bantam, 1974.

Garfield, Charles. *Peak Performers: The New Heroes of American Business.* New York: Avon, 1986.

Goldberg, Natalie. *Writing Down the Bones: Freeing the Writer Within.* Boston: Shambhala, 1986.

Gross, Ronald. *Peak Learning.* Los Angeles, CA: Jeremy P. Tarcher, Inc. 1991.

Herrigel, Eugen. *Zen in the Art of Archery.* New York: Vintage Books, 1971.

Hickman, Craig R., and Silva, Michael A. *Creating Excellence.* New York: New American Library, 1984.

Loehr, James E., and McLaughlin, Peter. *Mentally Tough.* New York: M. Evans & Co., Inc. 1986.

Orlick, Terry. *In Pursuit of Excellence.* 2nd ed. Champagne: Leisure Press, 1980.

Ramsland, Steven. "The Phenomenology of the Experience of Flow in Work." Ph.D. diss., Rutgers University, 1989.

Suzuki, D. T. *Zen and Japanese Culture.* New York: McGraw-Hill, 1956.

Creativity

Dorman, Leslie, and Ediden, Peter. "Original Spin." *Psychology Today,* (July/Aug 1989): pp. 48-52.

Perkins, D. N. *The Mind's Best Work.* Cambridge: Harvard University Press, 1981.

Raudsepp, Eugene. *More Creative Growth Games.* New York: G. P. Putnam's Sons, 1980.

Winner, Ellen. *Invented Worlds: The Psychology of the Arts.* Cambridge: Harvard University Press, 1982.

Personality Traits

Di Mattia, Dominic J., Yeager, Raymond, and Dube, Ilene. "Emotional Barriers to Learning." *Personal Journal,* (Nov 1989): pp. 86-89.

Finke, J. "Fear...the Enemy of Love and Learning." *Illinois Teacher of Home Economics.* 31 (May/Je 1988): 211-12.

Langer, Ellen J. *Mindfulness.* New York: Addison-Wesley, 1989.

Waitley, Denis. *The Psychology of Winning.* New York: Berkeley Books. 1979.

Waitley, Denis, and Witt, Reni L. *The Joy of Working.* New York: Ballantine, 1985.

Motivation/Learning

Barker, Philip. *Using Metaphors in Psychotherapy.* New York: Bruner/Mazel, 1985.

Berliner, D. "Helping Kids Learn How to Learn," *Instructor.* 99 (Jan 1990): 16-17.

Bowers. G. H., ed. "The Psychology of Learning and Motivation, 1990." *The Psychology of Learning and Motivation.* 24:1-341. 1989.

Csikszentmihalyi, Mihaly. "Education and Lifelong Learning." In R. Gross (ed.) *Invitation To Lifelong Learning.* New York: Follett, 1982.

Csikszentmihalyi, Mihaly. "Intrinsic Motivation and Effective Teaching." In J. Bess (ed.), *The Motivation to Teach.* San Francisco: Jossey-Bass, 1981.

Deci, E. L., and Ryan, R. M. *Intrinsic Motivation and Self-Determination in Human Behavior.* New York: Plenum, 1985.

Kantrowitz, Barbara, and Wingert, Pat. "How Kids Learn." *Newsweek,* April 17 1989, pp. 50-56.

Kiester, Edwin, Jr., and Kiester, Sally Valente. "How to Teach Your Child to Think." *Reader's Digest,* June, 1991, pp. 140-144.

Lewis, David, and Greene, James. *Thinking Better.* New York: Rawson, Wade, 1982.

Rosenthal, N. "Active Learning/Empowered Learning." *Adult Learning.* 1 (Fall 1990): 16-18.

Scott, Gini Graham. *Mind Power.* New Jersey: Prentice-Hall, 1987.

General/Theoretical

Bayles, Michael. *Professional Ethics.* Belmont: Wadsworth, 1981. (On types of relationships.)

Grinder, John, and Bandler, Richard. *Trance-Formations.* Utah: Real People Press, 1981. (on reframing).

de Saint Exupery, Antoine. *The Little Prince.* New York: Harcourt Brace Jovanovich, 1956. (on mental flexibility).

Heidegger, Martin. *Being and Time.* Translated by John Macquarrie and Edward Robinson. New York: Harper & Row, 1962.

Kierkegaard, Soren. *Concluding Unscientific Postscript.* Translated by David F. Swenson, and Walter Lowrie. Princeton: Princeton University Press, [1846], 1968. (on double reflection).

Pirsig, Robert M. *Zen and the Art of Motorcycle Maintenance.* New York: Bantam, 1974.

Plato, "The Republic" in *The Collected Dialogues.* Edith Hamilton and Huntington Cairns eds. Princeton, NJ: Princeton University Press, 1961.

Sartre, Jean-Paul. *Existentialism is a Humanism.* Translated by P. Mairet. The Philosophical Library, 1949.

Index